OAKE OF BRITTAYN

BIBLIA
SACRA

GALLEYWOOD

MAGNA CHARTA

Quercu cadente ligna quiuis colligit

30130 151763892

Fatted for

The English Civil War

www.pocketessentials.com

The following places and battles are marked on the map:

SCOTLAND

Berwick

Newcastle
Carlisle
Durham
Penrith
Appleby
Kendal

Marston Moor
Skipton
York
Preston
Leeds
Hull
Ardwalton Moor
Wakefield
Bolton
Manchester
Liverpool
Gainsborough
Chester
Lincoln
Winceby
Nantwich
Newark
Market Drayton
Burton upon Trent
Stafford
Ashby de la Zouch
Shrewsbury
Lichfield
Leicester
WALES
Naseby
Newmarket
Worcester
Evesham
Tewkesbury
Newport Pagnell
Hereford
Buckingham
Colchester
Gloucester
Edgehill
ENGLAND
Oxford
Pembroke
Abingdon
LONDON
Bristol
Lansdown
Reading
Roundway Down
Newbury
Maidstone
Langport
Salisbury
Taunton
Cheriton
Stratton
Shaftesbury
Arundel
Exeter
Lyme Regis
Weymouth
Lostwithiel
Plymouth

0   •   50
Miles

~Arthur Banks~

The Principal Battles and Places of the Civil War

The English Civil War

DAVID CLARK

POCKET ESSENTIALS

First published in 2008 by Pocket Essentials
P O Box 394, Harpenden, Herts, AL5 1XJ
www.pocketessentials.com

A CIP catalogue record for this book is available from the British Library.

ISBN 978-1-84243-293-8

2 4 6 8 10 9 7 5 3 1

Typeset by Avocet Typeset, Chilton, Aylesbury, Bucks
Printed and bound in Great Britain by
J.H.Haynes Ltd, Sparkford, Yeovil, Somerset

Contents

Introduction:
Playing the Game

This Kingdom hath been too long at peace.

Sir Edward Cecil, Viscount Wimbledon

The English Civil War was a conflict in which no one, especially the King, intended to play by the rules and, as such, it was said to mark the end of the age of chivalry. It was strictly a 'gloves off' contest. Many of the leading participants changed sides – often for gain – and those who remained loyal often went unrewarded by their masters. Those who had been impoverished by their support of Charles I would have to fight tooth and nail to win recognition and recompense from his son at the Restoration.

The objective of Parliament appeared to be simple enough: to capture the King to win. The problem was that the King could only be placed in check; he could not be removed from the board. No one had thought through the implications of the King's refusal to concede defeat. Sooner or later, it was thought, he had to see sense but, as far as he was concerned, his situation was non-negotiable: he had been appointed by God, and it was no man's business to dispute his Divine Right to rule as he saw fit.

The King's intransigence, from 1629 onwards, created a tense situation in which something had to give, and everybody wanted a piece of the action. Best placed to take advantage of the crisis were those close to the monarch, favourites such as the Duke of Buckingham had been. They often failed to perform their duties satisfactorily, but this was of secondary importance to their critics, whose main reason for resentment was the fact that they themselves were excluded from taking advantage of opportunities for personal profit afforded by appointment to high office.

Another major player with an eye for the main chance was the Queen. A practising Catholic, she was treated with suspicion by Parliamentarians and Royalists alike, for she would stop at nothing to promote the cause of Rome in her husband's realm. Like Margaret of Anjou, queen to King Henry VI, before her, Henrietta Maria provided the practical initiative that her husband lacked in rallying support for his cause. At one juncture, she toyed with the idea of fielding her own army – and a number of women did go so far as to take up arms. However, the heroism of most of the women whose stories have come down to us occurred within a conservative background of domesticity, as exemplified in the devotion to their husbands of Margaret, Duchess of Newcastle and Lucy Hutchinson, wife of Parliamentarian Colonel John Hutchinson, in times of great hardship.

Also close to the King was the Archbishop of Canterbury, William Laud. Just as the movement of a bishop on a chess board is restricted, so the power of senior clergy was limited – to matters ecclesiastical. Hearkening back to the days of Cardinal Wolsey, Laud wanted to extend this boundary, and he and his followers developed increasingly influential roles in secular affairs. As far as the Parliamentarians were concerned, episcopacy had to be eliminated. Throughout the war years, rarely did there appear a major piece of legislation which bore no reference to this priority.

In addition to Anglicans and Catholics, there were also the Puritans, for whom the Reformation had not gone far enough. Religion, they argued, was a personal matter, between worshipper and God; there was no need for a priesthood or elaborate rituals. Puritans were particularly active in Parliament and came to be identified as the voice of parliamentary opposition to the crown.

At least many of the knights, or landed gentry, played according to the rules. It was natural that they should do so, for their privileged way of life owed as much to the maintenance of the status quo as did that of the King. By giving their support to Charles, they could look forward to further preferment. Knights were elevated to the peerage and peers, in turn, promoted to dukes. Often, their tenants were treated like vassals. When war came, they were expected to follow their lords into battle, much as their ancestors had done in the days of the Wars of the Roses.

The pawns in the game were many. Some 80,000 combatants were killed over the period 1642–49, most of the bodies being interred in mass graves close to battlefields. The ordinary soldier cared little for whom he fought, and it was common practice for prisoners to agree to change sides and fight for their captors. Non-combatants normally made themselves agreeable to whichever army happened to be in the neighbourhood. Others, in remote locations, appeared not to know that a war was being fought. There is a story of a Long Marston farm labourer who, when asked whom he was for, King or Parliament, allegedly replied: 'What? Be them two fallen out, then?' In the final analysis, any Royalist, regardless of rank, could expect to be sacrificed in order to save the King. Thus, the Earl of Strafford went to the block to mollify the King's fiercest front-bench critics, while the Marquess of Montrose was condemned to death to facilitate Charles II's policy of appeasement towards his father's former enemies.

The key players were those who had no place on the board: the minor gentry who occupied the no-man's land between influence and obscurity, the sons of prosperous merchants or people like Oliver Cromwell, who described himself as 'by birth a gentleman living neither in any considerable height nor yet in obscurity'. They were 'electable', which is to say that they were able to stand for Parliament. But, once elected, they were unable to exert much influence. Of what use is a parliament which is created for a specific purpose at the behest of the King, and which is condemned to oblivion immediately afterwards? They liked to see themselves as crusaders, waging a holy war on behalf of the people they represented. To an extent this was true but, since most of the population did not have a vote, they represented a minority – a bigger minority than the one which was already clinging to power but a minority none the less. When they attained power, they pulled up the ladder very smartly. Everyone seeks an opportunity to strut and fret his hour upon the stage. It was their turn. This was their hour.

1634–37: The Board

I hope for blood sake he will be welcome, though I believe he will not much trouble the ladies with courting them, nor be thought a very 'beau garcon'... Give your good counsel to Rupert, for he is still a little giddy, though not so much as he has been. I pray tell him when he does ill, for he is good-natured enough, but doth not always think what he should do.

Letter from the Queen of Bohemia to Sir Henry Vane, written prior to Prince Rupert's first visit to England in February 1636

On 28 August 1628, a lieutenant of infantry named John Felton loitered nervously in the Greyhound Inn on Portsmouth's High Street. He stood apart from the general conviviality, for he had a very specific purpose in mind. He was there to kill a man. Despite the nature of his calling, he was armed only with a cheap knife, purchased at a cutler's shop on Tower Hill, but this mean weapon would do the job well enough, provided he kept his nerve. His meticulous planning even involved the preparation of a written confession, which he had sewed carefully into his hatband.

Passed over for promotion, owed some 80 pounds in back pay and still suffering from wounds received during an ill-fated expedition to La Rochelle, Felton bore a grudge against the man he considered responsible for all his misfortunes – and, indeed, for the woes of the English nation. There were many who would have agreed with him. As his unsuspecting quarry came into view, Felton lunged towards him, drew the knife and drove it deep into his heart. It all happened so quickly that the unfortunate individual could only gasp in astonishment before he fell to the floor, stone dead.

The assassination became international news, for the victim was George Villiers, Duke of Buckingham, favourite of King Charles I. Buckingham's enemies were legion and the authorities found it difficult to believe that Felton had acted alone. So lengthy was the subsequent investigation that it was three months before the accused was brought to trial. He was hanged at Tyburn and his body returned to Portsmouth where, in a display of medieval barbarity, it was hung in chains for the edification of the local populace.

The manner of Buckingham's death may have been unexpected, but his days of influence and power had been numbered even before he was assassinated. He had been responsible for abortive and disastrous conflicts with Spain and France and had been saved from impeachment only by the King's dissolution of Parliament earlier in the year. His demise did provide Charles with an opportunity to start over, and to ease the strained relations between the monarch and an increasingly fractious House of Commons. Although a number of the King's enemies did withdraw their opposition in exchange for preferment, both sides tended to become more firmly entrenched in their opposing views of how the country should be governed. Between March 1629 and April 1640, Charles chose to rule without calling a parliament, which was a considerable challenge, if only because parliaments constituted a monarch's main source of income. These years are known as the period of 'Personal Rule'.

Charles did not consider himself to be a despot, but he was a confirmed believer in the Divine Right of Kings. His was a mission entrusted to him by God, and he intended to see it through. His father, James I, had wrestled with the issues of religion and political opposition to kingship but, where James was shrewd, Charles was obstinate, lacking the qualities of statesmanship which would be needed to secure the survival of the monarchy in the troubled times which lay ahead. A Venetian diplomat wrote of him: 'This king is so constituted by nature, that he never obliges any one, either by word or deed.' Even his choice of a wife displayed a lack of tact. Originally, he had hoped to marry Maria, daughter of Philip III of Spain but, when the scheme fell through, he married Henrietta Maria, daughter of Henry IV of France. Both girls were devout Roman Catholics, illustrating Charles's toleration of the Catholic Church. Throughout the 1630s, Henrietta Maria increasingly interfered in affairs of state, creating, in the process, a number of powerful enemies in parliament.

King James's handling of successive parliaments had left much to be desired. Under Charles, an already strained relationship continued to decline. In exchange for personal favours, parliaments were supposed to grant a monarch the cash he required for anything from meeting his personal expenses to the prosecution of foreign wars. The five Parliaments called between 1621 and 1628 had stopped playing the game, the Members exhibiting a worrying tendency to criticise the King's policies, his ministers and the King himself. They even wanted a substantial share in the decision-making process.

Charles began to cast around for ways of securing an income without recourse to parliaments. He had already resorted to a forced loan, by which everyone liable to parliamentary taxation was compelled to tender a contribution. With the aid of one of his reformed critics, William Noy, he now resurrected a number of obsolete laws, such as that which required every man who possessed an estate worth at least £40 per annum to take up a knighthood. Penalties totalling £175,000 were levied against those who had failed to comply. Medieval laws governing forests were also revived, which meant that landowners who had encroached on what had once been royal forests were heavily fined.

Another promising earner involved the sale of monopolies in everything from brick-making to coal-shipping. One company received a patent for making – and a monopoly for selling – soap. The company comprised friends of Richard Weston, the then Lord Treasurer, who happened to be Catholics. The commodity gained notoriety as 'Popish Soap'. One of the most unpopular taxes through which Charles sought to increase his income was 'Ship Money'. It was not a new tax; it had been levied on various ports and coastal counties for the purposes of naval defence in times of war. In 1634, however, ship-money was demanded from all the maritime counties. It brought in over £100,000, encouraging the King to extend it the following year to all the inland counties as well.

Among those who refused to pay was Buckinghamshire landowner, Justice of the Peace and experienced parliamentarian, John Hampden. Under the provisions of the ship-money tax, Buckinghamshire was required to provide a ship of 450 tons, together with cannon and a full crew – or else pay the sum of £4,500. One wonders what would have happened if the county had called the King's bluff and produced the vessel instead of the cash. However, Hampden threw down the gauntlet. The tax, he argued, was being levied without the consent of Parliament and, as such, was illegal. Opposition to the tax was growing. Even loyal Royalists such as Yorkshireman Sir Marmaduke Langdale, who would become one of the King's stoutest supporters during the Civil War, refused to pay. Charles asked the Lord Chief Justice, Sir John Finch, for a ruling. Finch decreed that in times of peril, His Majesty would be justified in extending the tax to the country at large. Most of the defaulters climbed down, leaving only a handful of recalcitrant rebels, of whom Hampden was one.

Having himself taken legal advice, Hampden resolved to stand firm. The tax amounted to only twenty shillings (£1) on his Stoke Mandeville estate, but on this paltry sum was fought one of the most celebrated trials of the age. By the time the case came to court in November 1637, Hampden was known throughout the land. The arguments were simple enough. For Hampden, it was argued that there were no national security issues which warranted the King's action: it had been a decision for Parliament. For the Crown, the Solicitor-General built his case around the principle of Divine Right: the nation had been entrusted to His Majesty's care by God, and he reported to God alone. The King was expected to win, and he did – but only by the narrowest of margins. Of the twelve judges, five were for Hampden.

Far more socially divisive than the taxation issue was that of religion. Presiding over the Church of England was the Archbishop of Canterbury, William Laud, appointed in 1633. The son of a Reading clothier, Laud has been described as the most hated archbishop in English history. After his death, it was said of him that 'he intended the discipline of the church should be felt, as well as spoken of', and he did, indeed, impose his iron will upon congregations throughout the land. As a self-made man, it was, perhaps, natural that Laud should also subscribe to the doctrine of free-will, but he was careful to ensure that anyone else who sought preferment towed the line. Five specific examples of Laud's tyranny are usually quoted: those of Leighton, Prynne, Bastwick, Burton and Lilburne.

Alexander Leighton was a Scot, a theologian who penned a 'seditious' volume entitled *Zion's Plea against Prelacy*, roundly condemning the power of the bishops in the Church. Found guilty of 'anti-Christian and satanic' practices, he was publicly whipped, branded on the face with the letters 'SS' (Sower of Sedition) and had his ears cut off. In 1634, William Prynne, a lawyer, suffered a similar fate for a thinly disguised attack on Queen Henrietta Maria. Initially, his ears were only partially cropped, but three years later, the stumps were removed and he was branded on the cheeks with the letters 'SL' (Seditious Libeller). Two other writers of controversial pamphlets, Henry Burton and John Bastwick, also lost their ears, while the fifth, John Lilburne, suffered the indignity of being tied to a cart-tail and whipped from the Fleet to the Palace Yard in Westminster, before being pilloried. Instead of stamping out the problem, however, Laud's policy of repression merely led to an increase in the amount of subversive literature hitting the streets.

Laud's enemies categorised him as an adherent of 'Arminianism' (from the theologian, Joseph Arminius) which emphasised the importance of the ceremonial aspects of worship. He relished what he called 'the external worship of God in His Church', and described ceremonies and rituals as 'the hedge that fence the substance of religion from all the indignities which profaneness and sacrilege too commonly put upon it'. The altar was to be placed at the east end of the church and railed off. Statues of the Virgin Mary and the Saints were imported and new stained-glass windows installed – suggesting a definite bias towards the Church of Rome. In fact, although Laud's actions were a response to the rising tide of Puritanism, he also had little sympathy with the Catholics. He went so far as to ask the King to restrict the number of conversions to Catholicism – a move which was vetoed by the Queen.

In fairness, it must be said that Laud accomplished much good. Before his coming, there was much disorder in Church affairs; some clergy neglected their duties and many churches were dirty and decayed. Cock-fights were staged in churches and St Paul's Cathedral doubled as the Stock Exchange. Although Laud put an end to such practices, it was inevitable that his reactionary policies would put him on a collision course with the Puritans, who wished to purge the Church of England of what they regarded as superstitious and corrupt observances retained after the severance from Rome.

Laud's political influence grew, his supporters securing several important positions. In particular, when the position of Lord High Treasurer became vacant in 1636, it was Laud's influence which led to the appointment of William Juxon, Bishop of London, to the post – with the added position of Lord of the Admiralty thrown in. The Puritans, who counted many prominent parliamentarians among their number, had a potentially strong political base but, as long as Charles could manage without calling a parliament, they were powerless for, in all cases, the law favoured the King.

Of especial use to Charles during his period of 'Personal Rule' was the so-called Star Chamber. This had its origins in the fifteenth century and was intended to ensure fair play in cases involving powerful magnates who stood little chance of being convicted of their crimes by lesser courts. It could also be used to try cases of sedition, as in the trials of the five men who incurred Laud's displeasure. There is little wonder that it developed a reputation as a tool for delivering oppression. Working in tandem with the Star Chamber was the Court of High Commission, an ecclesiastical court set up in 1580. It had always been used to coerce Puritans into conformity, in particular by means of the ex-officio oath, through which those called before it could be forced to give evidence against themselves. Those who refused to take the oath were turned over to the Star Chamber.

Sir Thomas Wentworth in the secular sphere was as hated as Laud was in the ecclesiastical. A leading Parliamentarian, he changed sides and, in 1628, was appointed President of the Council of the North. To all intents and purposes, he *was* the law in the North of England, and he was determined never to let anyone forget it. Like Laud (the two men got on famously), Wentworth was a gifted administrator and, also like Laud, he accomplished much good. As a Poor Law Commissioner, for example, he was instrumental in enforcing the Elizabethan Poor Law at local level and thus relieving much social distress. The downside of his position was that he was far removed from life at Court, and was therefore unable to challenge his enemies.

This geographical isolation became even more pronounced when he was appointed Lord Deputy of Ireland. When he took over, Irish affairs were in a deplorable state.

There was no money with which to pay the army, there was a dire shortage of arms and ammunition and Dublin Castle, the Governor's residence, was in a ruinous condition. So neglected was the administration that the seals of office were still in the name of James I. To cap it all, in sight of Dublin, a ship carrying Wentworth's luggage was casually taken by pirates.

The new Lord Deputy faced a number of complex problems. Ireland was in constant turmoil, the scene of an ongoing struggle between the native Irish Catholics, the 'old' English Catholics, led by the Earl of Ormonde, and the 'new' English – Protestants who had settled on land taken from Irish Catholics. Wentworth set to work to tackle corruption in the government at Dublin, strengthened the Protestant Church of Ireland and reorganised the Irish army. When he took over, Ireland was a drain on the Treasury but, under his supervision, the revenues due to – and successfully collected for – the Crown increased dramatically.

Undeniably, Wentworth benefited from his work, acquiring some 59,000 acres of land and amassing a personal annual income of £23,000. The fact that his predecessors had also helped themselves was forgotten. More disturbingly, he intended to continue the policy of confiscating land belonging to Catholics and turning it over to Protestants, as a means of transforming Ireland into a Protestant country.

Together, Wentworth and Laud implemented what they called the policy of 'Thorough' – a term which probably originated with Wentworth and which seemed to carry an implication of absolutism. Certainly Laud wrote to Wentworth on one occasion, expressing his hope that his ally would make himself 'as absolute in Ireland as any prince in the whole world'. Whatever he did, Wentworth was bound to be the focus of resentment. He had inherited the mantle of Buckingham and, in so doing, was transformed into 'Black Tom Tyrant', the man everybody loved to hate – and the prime target of his late colleagues in parliament.

The political and religious problems of the nation were exacerbated by trying economic conditions, for these were years of food shortages and rising prices. A series of poor harvests increased the risk of death by starvation and lowered resistance to common diseases such as pneumonia and consumption. Industrially, too, England was under threat. The woollen industry began to suffer from foreign competition and a decline in European demand for traditional broadcloth. In addition, the Dutch were proving particularly bullish in the competitive business of establishing trading interests overseas.

Such was the state of affairs when the crisis which would send the nation careering towards civil war was brewing north of the border in Scotland. Charles himself was a Scot, having been born in Dunfermline, but he knew little of the country and still less of its people. On his succession, he decreed that 'matters shall continue and go forward in the same course wherein they are now' – a statement which summed up his entire philosophy of life.

1638–41: The Bishops' Wars

*Sir, my consent shall more acquit you herein to God than all the
world can do besides. To a willing man there is no injury done, and as
by God's grace I forgive all the world with a calmness and meekness of
infinite contentment to my dislodging soul, so, sir, to you I can give
the life of the world with all the cheerfulness imaginable, in the just
acknowledgement of your exceeding favours*

From a letter written to King Charles I by the Earl of
Strafford from the Tower of London

Measures, however draconian, which the English people were
prepared to grin and bear, were flatly rejected by the Scots,
who added a nationalistic fervour to the unstable mixture of
religious and civil authoritarianism. With remarkable
sangfroid, Laud imposed upon Scotland a modified version of
the English Book of Common Prayer before its publication. Its
arrival in Edinburgh in May 1637 occasioned riots, in which
women played a leading role. In the coming months,
opposition grew more organised, and Charles was told plainly
that if he wanted his Prayer Book, he would have to back its
introduction with an army of 40,000 men.

In February 1638, the Scots drew up the Scottish National
Covenant, which unified national resistance to the
introduction of the Book of Common Prayer. The Kirk of
Scotland, it was averred, constituted 'the only true faith and

religion'. A vitriolic diatribe against the 'Roman Antichrist', the Covenant riled against such evils as the 'blasphemous priesthood', the 'worshipping of imagery, relics and crosses', 'praying or speaking in a strange language' and the 'blasphemous opinion of transubstantiation'. Included within the text was an assurance that the Covenanters (as they would be known) posed no threat to 'the King's greatness and authority', but that they would 'stand to the defence of our dread Sovereign the King's Majesty... in the defence and preservation of the aforesaid true religion, liberties and laws of the kingdom.' Presumably, should he falter in his commitment to the 'true religion', the subscribers would no longer consider their pledge to be binding.

During the summer of 1638, Charles considered taking immediate military action against the Scots. This, in itself, demonstrated an inability to face facts, for he had no army and, despite his fundraising activities, no money with which to acquire one. In the end he temporised, suspending the ecclesiastical reform programme until all the issues had been considered by a General Assembly of the Kirk. Packed with Covenanters, the Assembly met on 21 November 1638. Its achievements included the deposition and excommunication of bishops, censorship of the free press and the prohibition of salmon fishing on Sundays. Charles would have to back down or implement his will by force of arms.

The Royalist faction in Scotland proved to be no match for the Covenanters and so an English army – ultimately 20,000 strong, albeit undisciplined and poorly equipped – was cobbled together in the northern counties. In response, the Scots amassed an army which, although smaller, was trained by the experienced Alexander Leslie, who had seen active service on the European mainland. Charles sent his army to

Berwick, joining it on 30 May 1639. The plan was that his man in Scotland, the Marquess of Hamilton, would effect a diversion by taking 5,000 men to Aberdeen by sea. The planned landing never came off, while the few Royalist garrisons in Scotland offered only feeble resistance.

Leslie had marched to Duns Law, about twelve miles to the west of Berwick, where he halted. Neither side wanted to fight. With the English army were a great many men who feared that a victory for the King would merely strengthen his hand, while Leslie knew that a victory for the Scots might galvanise the spirit of English opposition. The waiting game suited Leslie, for Charles still lacked the funds to maintain his army. On 4 June, a day that was described as the hottest in living memory, the Earl of Holland, leading 3,000 horse and 2,000 foot, advanced across the border. Owing to the excessive heat, the infantry fell way behind the cavalry so that, when the enemy was sighted, the infantry, together with the artillery, was three or four miles in the rear. Holland could have waited for them to come up without fear of having to withstand an attack, but he lost his nerve and beat a hasty retreat to rejoin his infantry and fall back on Berwick. Charles had no choice but to agree to a cessation of hostilities.

On 18 June, a treaty known as the 'Pacification of Berwick' was signed. Charles was to ratify the findings of the Assembly in an English Parliament to be called in July – which would entail confirming the excommunication of the bishops. All 'matters ecclesiastical' were, in future, to be decided by Scottish General Assemblies, the English army was to be withdrawn and the Scots compensated.

It is said that a man is as good as his word and, over the coming decade, Charles would show time and again that he was not to be trusted. He had no intention of sticking to the terms of the treaty which he had just negotiated, although after ruling for so long without recourse to a parliament, he now decided to call one. This assembly would become known as the 'Short Parliament', because it met for only three weeks, from 13 April 1640.

After eleven years of suppression, the Members were hardly likely to harbour any feelings of magnanimity towards the Crown, yet Charles thought that he could bargain his way into a position where they would vote to grant him around £750,000, so that hostilities with the Scots could be renewed on a more secure footing. Instead, John Pym, the leading voice of dissent, merely waxed lyrical on the subject of the nation's ecclesiastical and civil grievances. This hostility was conveyed to the King. Indeed, it was suggested by contemporaries that he received 'a worse representation of the humour and affection of the house than it deserved', implying that, given more time, it may have been possible to reach an accommodation. Nevertheless, on 5 May, the Parliament was peremptorily dissolved.

The Earl of Strafford – as Wentworth, in recognition of his services to the crown, had now become – advised his master to move against the Scots swiftly, and strike a decisive blow which would leave no one in any doubt as to who was in charge. He is alleged to have said: 'Your Majesty has an army in Ireland which may help you to reduce this kingdom.' To which 'kingdom' was he referring, his critics wanted to know? Did he mean that he planned to use an Irish Catholic army to quell dissent in England?

Charles produced his begging bowl. Strafford set an example by contributing £20,000. Others followed suit and within three weeks £300,000 was raised. An army was assembled and placed under the command of the Earl of Northumberland. In one respect, it was the right choice, for the Earls of Northumberland had borne the brunt of Scottish incursions for centuries. Unfortunately, Northumberland fell ill almost immediately and asked to be relieved. Charles sent for Strafford, who had returned to Ireland, but he, too, was incapacitated. Increasingly severe attacks of gout had all but crippled him and, although he made his best speed, he arrived too late to avert disaster.

Strafford was appointed Commander-in-Chief of the King's army on 3 August, but the Scots were already on the march. By the end of July, Leslie was preparing to invade England. For some time, the most radical of the Parliamentarians had been in touch with the Scots, promising (treasonably) their support. On 20 August, Leslie reached the River Tweed. The Earl of Montrose, accompanying him, set an example to the men by wading across the Tweed on foot — not that they needed much encouragement to prosecute what they considered to be a Holy War. A small English force, sent out from Berwick to impede Leslie's steady progress towards Newcastle, was brushed aside.

Arriving at Newburn, ten miles from his objective, on 27 August, Leslie encountered a stronger force of some 3,000 foot and 1,500 horse, which had advanced from Newcastle under the command of Lord Conway, and which was drawn up on the south bank of the River Tyne. The Newburn ford was one of several fording points along the Tyne, but it was the lowest and, during what was a very wet summer, it was the most practicable place to cross.

In fact, there would have been no need for Leslie to cross the river at all but, although anxious to press on to

Newcastle, he could not risk being taken in the rear, should the English decide to cross over to the north bank and follow him in. Fortunately, his army was 20,000 strong and he could afford to divide it. One division, under Montrose, pushed on to Newcastle while Leslie remained at Newburn with the other.

As darkness fell, Leslie occupied the high ground above the village, concealing his artillery amid the ragged bushes covering the hillside. He had been short of artillery but had been able to improvise, thanks to a stratagem which he had learned in Germany, involving the manufacture of temporary small calibre cannon. Capable of firing only a few rounds before bursting, they could still help in giving the enemy a misleading impression of the strength of an army's firepower. A few guns were also placed on the tower of the Norman church.

During the morning of 28 August, the armies faced one another, neither overtly anxious to make the first move. According to tradition, hostilities began with the action of a single, foolhardy Scot, who advanced to the river – perhaps only to water his horse. He was shot dead. In the artillery exchange that followed, the English – their guns mounted on hastily constructed breastworks – came off worst. Their undisciplined gun crews, overawed at the seemingly superior firepower of the Scots, abandoned their positions.

Realising that this could be the right time to attempt a crossing, Leslie sent a party of cavalry to test the water. They crossed without difficulty, giving Leslie sufficient confidence to start sending over his infantry. The English horse, thrown into disarray by the thunder of Leslie's guns, failed to respond. While contemporary English accounts of the battle tend to tone down the extent of the panic within the ranks, there is little doubt that Conway's men were soon in full flight.

Conway was accused of cowardice and threw the blame on his recruits, whom he described as 'the meanest sort of men about London' — which was probably true. Charles retreated to York while Leslie, approaching Newcastle, could hardly believe his luck when he discovered that the English garrison had abandoned the city. The populace welcomed the Scots who, instead of indulging in an orgy of pillage, behaved remarkably well.

In desperation, the King summoned a Grand Council of Peers of the Realm to meet at York, where commissioners were appointed to treat with the Scots. On 26 October, by the Treaty of Ripon, the Scots took temporary possession of the counties of Northumberland and Durham and, pending the conclusion of a final settlement, were to be paid £850 per day for the maintenance of their army while it remained on English soil.

In order to meet this potentially crippling expenditure, Charles had no choice but to call a parliament. Pym intended to make sure that it would be packed with opposition Members and embarked on a round of vigorous electioneering. The new parliament met on 3 November 1640 and is known as the 'Long Parliament' because it sat for the next twenty years.

A few far-sighted individuals may have experienced unease at the strong-arm tactics employed by Pym to ensure victory in the marginals, but his efforts bore fruit to the extent that the newly elected opposition overwhelmed the Royalists. It was a minor miracle that Pym himself had lasted for so long. His predecessor as acknowledged leader of the opposition, Sir John Eliot, had died a prisoner in the Tower in 1632, but Pym survived to 'sweep the house clean below' and 'to pull down all the cobwebs in the tops and corners'.

The House of Commons now had the upper hand and wallowed unashamedly in its newly acquired power. Laud was arrested and confined to the Tower of London, exchanging places with a number of his victims, including Prynne and his colleagues, who were freed. The Commons also entertained 'The Root and Branch Petition' from 'His Majesty's subjects in and about London, and several Counties of the Kingdom', on the topic of Church reform – in particular, the abolition of episcopacy. The removal of bishops from Church government would figure prominently in parliamentary debates in the coming years. On 15 February 1641, the Triennial Act was passed, aimed at 'the preventing of inconveniences happening by the long intermission of Parliaments'. Henceforth, parliaments would have to meet – if necessary, without royal authority – for a minimum of fifty days at least once every three years. Tucked in neatly at the end was a proviso that 'His Majesty's assent to this Bill shall not thereby determine this present Session of Parliament'.

It was only a matter of time before the Earl of Strafford was impeached on a charge of high treason and, in March 1641, he was brought to trial. Hitherto, treason could be committed only against the monarch but, in a new departure, Strafford was accused of attempting to overthrow the laws of the kingdom and to destroy the liberties of its subjects. His trial lasted for three weeks, but the evidence against him was so flimsy that the charges could not be made to stick. Even so, Pym was loath to retreat and rushed through the Commons a Bill of Attainder which was enacted on 10 May. The Bill repeated Strafford's alleged offences which, it was noted, 'hath been sufficiently proved against the said Earl upon his impeachment' and stipulated that for his 'heinous crimes', he should 'suffer such pains of death, and incur the forfeitures of his goods, chattels, lands, tenements and hereditaments'.

Surprisingly, the Bill also got through the House of Lords – placing Charles, who had promised to stand by Strafford, in a dilemma. He went so far as to offer £20,000 to Sir William Balfour, Lieutenant of the Tower of London, where Strafford languished, to allow his prisoner to escape. Like all his underhand dealings, the plan fell through and it was Strafford himself who let him off the hook by generously freeing him of his obligation, 'for prevention of evils which may happen by your refusal to pass this bill'. Strafford went to the block on 12 May.

Pym had got into his stride, and Acts of Parliament designed to limit royal power, while extending the power of Parliament, flowed thick and fast. Also on 10 May came an act prolonging the life of the Parliament indefinitely. Based upon the argument that time was needed to put the affairs of the nation in order, it was decreed that 'this present Parliament now assembled shall not be dissolved unless it be by an Act of Parliament to be passed for that purpose… and in like manner, that the House of Commons shall not, at any time or times, during this present Parliament be adjourned unless it be by themselves'.

There followed the 'Tonnage and Poundage Act', granting the King a tax on imports and exports, but there was a sting in its tail, for it included a timely reminder that 'it is and hath been the ancient right of the subjects of this realm, that no subsidy, custom, impost, or other charge whatsoever ought or may be laid or imposed upon any merchandise exported or imported by subjects, denizens, or aliens without common consent in Parliament'. On 7 August, there was passed an Act 'for the declaring unlawful and void the late proceedings touching Ship-money', through which the judgement against Hampden was set aside. Forest boundaries were restored, and there was an Act for 'the prevention of vexatious proceedings touching the Order of Knighthood'. In short, all the King's schemes for raising money without the consent of Parliament were scrapped.

Neither was the legal system forgotten. The Star Chamber was abolished – 'absolutely dissolved, taken away and determined'. No freeman was to be 'imprisoned, or disseized of his freehold or liberties or free customs, or be outlawed or exiled or otherwise destroyed', nor be condemned except by 'lawful judgement of his Peers or by the law of the land'. The Court of High Commission went the same way, with the decree that 'no new Court shall be erected, ordained or appointed... which shall or may have the like power, jurisdiction or authority as the said High Commission Court now hath or pretendeth to have'.

In an effort to escape from these indignities, Charles travelled to Scotland. En route, he encountered Alexander Leslie, who assured him of his loyalty and received a peerage, becoming Earl of Leven. In Edinburgh, the King presided over the Scottish Parliament and, in the mistaken belief that it was possible to please all Scotsmen all of the time, did his best to make himself agreeable to all and sundry. Leslie's army returned to Scotland and Charles convinced himself that, should the occasion arise, it would be placed at his disposal.

In his absence, the reform programme continued unabated. On 1 September, with a degree of clarity unknown in parliamentary language before or since, the House set forth its 'Resolutions on Ecclesiastical Innovations'. Churchwardens were directed to 'remove the communion table from the east end of the church... into some other convenient place'. All 'crucifixes, scandalous pictures of any one or more persons of the Trinity, and all images of the Virgin Mary' were to be removed. Sundays were to be 'observed and sanctified', while 'dancing or other sports, either before or after divine service' were to be 'forborne and restrained'. All of these reforms were to be implemented within a period of six weeks.

While the Parliamentarians were locked in an ivory tower of reforming zeal during the summer months of 1641, trouble was brewing in Ireland. In the absence of Strafford, the administration fell apart. The Irish army was disbanded and several clans, under the leadership of Phelim O'Neill, seized the opportunity to rise in revolt against their Protestant oppressors. Reports coming out of Ireland were sketchy, but it was claimed that 3,000 Protestants (1 in 5 of the population) had been massacred. With some justification, the Catholic rebels feared the supremacy of Puritanism in England and Scotland, while the Puritans viewed the rebellion as a Catholic conspiracy, designed to bring about their downfall.

Charles left Scotland on 17 November, his return journey being stage-managed to illustrate the loyalty of his subjects. In Ware, for example, he stopped and chatted with the local gentry and freeholders. There was a well-publicised reunion with the Queen and her children, and an enthusiastic welcome in London, where he was met by cheering crowds. He delivered a speech in which he promised future prosperity, and undertook to protect the Protestant religion.

All was set fair, it seemed, for a new beginning with King, Parliament and People working together – if not in harmony, then at least in a spirit of mutual toleration.

1642: Opening Gambits

Oh Lord, Thou knowest how busy I must be this day. If I forget thee,
do not Thou forget me.

Sir Jacob Astley, before the Battle of Edgehill

While the King and the People appeared to be on good
terms, Pym refused to play ball. It may be wondered why
Parliament had not used the opportunity of Charles's absence
in Scotland to push through some particularly insidious
challenge to his authority. In fact, an attempt had been made
with a weighty 'Grand Remonstrance' – consisting of 204
clauses – debated in the Lower Chamber while he was
travelling back to London. When put to the vote, it scraped
through by 159 votes to 148. Although it was not put to the
Lords, Pym contrived, somewhat unconstitutionally, to have
the document printed and circulated.

It was presented to Charles on 1 December – prefaced by
a statement in which Parliament expressed its 'thankfulness
and joy' in the King's 'safe and peaceable return out of
Scotland'. There were three major demands. First (and
foremost), the bishops must be deprived of their votes in
Parliament and steps taken to curb their 'immoderate
power'. Second, the King must 'vouchsafe to employ such
persons in your great and public affairs, and to take such to
be near you in places of trust, as your Parliament may have

cause to confide in'. Third, the King 'will be pleased to forbear to alienate any of the forfeited and escheated lands in Ireland which shall accrue to your crown by reason of this rebellion'.

On 23 December, the King gave his reply. He confirmed his wish to preserve 'the peace and safety of this kingdom from the design of the Popish party' and agreed to remove any 'illegal innovations' which may have crept into the Church, but he reminded Parliament that the bishops' right to vote in Parliament was founded on 'fundamental law'. He rejected the demand that the appointment of Ministers of State should be subject to Parliamentary approval, insisting that it was the 'undoubted right of the Crown of England to call such persons to our secret counsels, to public employment and our particular service as we shall think fit'. With regard to Ireland, he questioned whether it would be 'seasonable' to declare resolutions such as had been suggested 'before the events of a war be seen'.

It was a measured response and, as such, infuriated Pym. After Christmas, he renewed his attacks and, it is believed, started rumours that the Queen was about to be impeached. Charles, meanwhile, was laying his own trap for the handful of Parliamentarians he considered were responsible for the deteriorating situation, and went so far as to replace the Lord Lieutenant of the Tower with a dependable Royalist, Sir John Byron.

On 3 January 1642, Charles made his move. The Attorney-General, Sir Edward Herbert, appeared in the House of Lords and attempted to impeach Lord Kimbolton and five members of the House of Commons: Denzil Holles, Sir Arthur Haselrig, John Pym, John Hampden and William Strode. All were alleged to have 'traitorously endeavoured to subvert the fundamental laws and government of the kingdom of England, to deprive the King of his regal power' and 'traitorously endeavoured to subvert the rights and the very being of Parliaments'. Kimbolton (better known as the Earl of Manchester, to which title he succeeded in November 1642) was recognised as the leading Puritan in the Upper Chamber; Holles and Strode, leading radicals, had already been imprisoned for their opposition to the King, Strode for a period of eleven years; Haselrig had been particularly hostile towards Strafford and Laud; Hampden and Pym were obvious choices.

The Lords merely appointed a committee to consider the matter. Charles ordered the Serjeant-at-Arms to arrest the five Commoners, but the House refused to surrender them. It is said that, in response, Henrietta Maria advised Charles to arrest the five Commoners in person, telling him to 'pull out those rogues by the ears'. Accordingly, on the afternoon of 4 January, the dutiful husband, accompanied by a motley assortment of armed supporters, described as 'soldiers, Papists and others', invaded the Commons, but to no avail for the accused were absent. Having been forewarned of the plan, 'the birds were flown' as Charles himself put it. When he enquired as to their whereabouts, the Speaker, William Lenthall, famously replied: 'I have neither eyes to see, nor tongue to speak in this place but as this House is pleased to direct me.'

In all probability, the King would have been surprised if the five members had, indeed, been awaiting his arrival. Had their arrest been top of the agenda, then they could have been taken into custody individually, in a number of alternative locations. By marching into the Lower Chamber, Charles was simply reinforcing a point: that Parliament sat and functioned at his behest. Nevertheless, he had played into Pym's hands. Against the advice of his supporters, he now committed an even more serious error of judgement. On 10 January, he abandoned London for Hampton Court.

The torrent of increasingly vitriolic legislation continued. On 13 February came the Clerical Disabilities Act, which stated that henceforth, bishops would not 'have any seat or place, suffrage, or voice, or use, or execute any power or authority in the Parliaments of this realm'. On the same day, there was the Impressment Act 'for the raising and levying of soldiers for the present defence of the kingdoms of England and Ireland'. War now seemed inevitable and, towards the end of the month, the Queen left the country, in part for her own safety but also with the aim of canvassing support in Europe.

On 3 March, Charles set out for York. He was prepared to sacrifice the bishops, but he could hardly be expected to sanction an Act to raise an army which could be used against him. Two days later, Parliament issued a 'Militia Ordinance' of doubtful legality. Ostensibly it was 'for the safety of His Majesty's person' but it had the effect of placing the country on a war footing. It was during disturbances arising from the Militia Ordinance that the English Civil War claimed its first casualty with the death of a Manchester linen weaver, Richard Perceval. Wounded on 15 July, he died a few days later.

The Royal progress to York was leisurely, but there was an important stop to be made at Hull, where arms and ammunition had been stored at the conclusion of the Bishops' Wars. Charles needed them, but he suffered a further indignity when he arrived to find Hull's Beverley Gate closed to him. He spent a full day making pleas and threats, but the Governor, Sir John Hotham, stood firm, and Charles had to turn for York in the knowledge that the arsenal could be used against him by his enemies.

On 1 June, Parliament made what it claimed to be a conciliatory gesture in a document entitled 'The Nineteen Propositions', outlining the usual demands – with which the King, by this time, must have been well acquainted. In case he were tempted to concede, a few additional 'humble desires', which he would be sure to reject, were appended. Kimbolton and the five members of the Commons were to be cleared of any wrongdoing; the 'military forces now attending Your Majesty' must be 'removed and discharged'; the Militia Ordinance must be approved. As a final humiliation, Parliament stipulated that it must approve of 'the government and education of the King's children', and that no marriage must be concluded for them without Parliamentary approval.

The King's answer was to issue his own Commissions of Array, requiring his loyal subjects to muster and train 'all the ancient trained bands and freehold bands... carefully seeing that they be supplied with able and sufficient persons, and completely armed'. On 12 July, Parliament voted to raise an army – again 'for the safety of the King's person' – of which 'the Earl of Essex shall be general'.

To an extent, both sides depended upon private capital to finance their war efforts. Charles was very reliant upon the wealthy Royalist magnates, who put armies, large and small, in the field at their own expense. While Parliament levied taxes to support its troops, the men often went unpaid and looked to their Generals for sustenance. In the beginning, only limited efforts were made to mobilise on a national basis, for it was felt that a single set-piece battle would settle the issue. This war, it was thought, as it has been thought of so many others before and since, would be over by Christmas.

The Royal Standard was raised at Nottingham on 22 August 1642. (Later, it blew down – an ill omen, if ever there was one.) As his Commander-in-Chief, Charles had appointed the Earl of Lindsey, who was a valuable asset. Like the Earl of Leven, Lindsey had fought in Europe, but he had a tough job, for Charles, who often accompanied his troops in the field, would make his own strategic decisions. By the autumn, when the Royalist army was around 15,000 strong, Lindsey had already resigned following an altercation with Prince Rupert, who was appointed General of Horse. Sir Jacob Astley, already 63 years old, was appointed Sergeant-Major-General of Infantry.

Prince Rupert was the King's nephew, offspring of the marriage of Charles's sister and Frederick III of the Palatinate, a German state. Together with his younger brother, Prince Maurice, he had travelled to England to assist his uncle in the defence of his throne. An expert horseman, Rupert had military experience and talent, but he had also inherited the Stuart trait of superciliousness. He took orders from no one but Charles and, in any argument, whenever push came to shove, his uncle would take his side. It was Rupert who would see the first action of the war. There had been desultory fighting throughout the summer, notably in the vicinity of Hull, with its coveted arsenal, but the first acknowledged battle took place at Powick Bridge, near Worcester.

At the suggestion of Bishop Prideaux of Worcester, who was Vice-Chancellor of the University of Oxford, the Oxford Colleges offered their plate to the King. A regiment of dragoons was sent to Oxford to collect it and convoy it to the Royal Mint at Aberystwyth. This regiment, one of six provided by the Earl of Worcester, was commanded by Sir John Byron. Byron reached Worcester, occupying it on 16 September, and Rupert was sent to reinforce him. Essex was also en route to Worcester, reaching Pershore, six miles to the south-east, on 21 September. There he halted, sending forward a detachment of horse under Captain Nathaniel Fiennes to monitor Byron's movements. Fiennes established himself at Powick, where he was beset by sightseers anxious to 'see the soldiers'.

On 23 September, a rumour to the effect that Byron was on the move reached the camp and Fiennes set out for Worcester to intercept him. He marshalled his men on meadows between the village of Powick and the River Teme. They crossed the narrow Powick Bridge and had gone only a short distance when they suddenly encountered Prince Rupert, who had arrived the previous day to cover Byron's march. It was a hot afternoon and Rupert and his men were taking their ease in the shade. Both sides were surprised by the encounter. Fiennes had the advantage of being on the move but, before he realised what was happening, the Royalists had mounted up and were bearing down upon him. Another version of the story has Rupert ready and waiting for Fiennes, who was allowed to cross the bridge. Whatever the truth of the matter, the fight lasted about a quarter of an hour and Fiennes, with the narrow bridge behind him, was unable to organise his troops to meet the attack, which led to Rupert winning the day. All the Royalist officers except Rupert were wounded and up to fifty Parliamentarians were killed. The remainder retired in disorder. Rupert failed to pursue them beyond Powick, enabling Parliament to make an absurd claim that the encounter had been a victory. Byron got through with his convoy and Rupert had established his reputation as a cavalry commander.

The Earl of Essex reached Worcester the following day and the city surrendered to him without resistance. The cathedral was used to stable horses and the organs and vestments were destroyed, while the Parliamentarian dragoons, clad in surplices, danced in the streets. Not everyone was so enthralled. Perhaps with the debacle at Powick Bridge in mind, Oliver Cromwell remarked on the disparity between the cavalry of the two armies, observing to Hampden that the Parliamentarian army was composed largely of 'old decayed serving men and tapsters'.

Allowing for the minor action at Powick Bridge, and sundry clashes of arms in other parts of the country, the war in the autumn of 1642 was still a 'phony' war. Neither side had fully organised or taken advantage of any form of military intelligence. Thus, the Royalists were unaware of Essex's strength while, for his part, Essex had little idea of the King's movements. Therefore, although Charles struck camp at Shrewsbury on 12 October, intending to march on London, Essex made no attempt to intercept him until a week later, leaving Worcester on 19 October.

On 22 October, the Royalists arrived at Edgcote, to the north-east of Banbury. Essex was only twelve miles to the west, at Kineton, and both sides intended using Wormleighton, midway between Edgcote and Kineton, to billet some of their men. It was not until troops ran into each other in the village that either side became aware of the other's proximity. Rupert supported the notion of attacking immediately, counting on the element of surprise to strike a decisive blow. Another option was to make a run for it, trusting to luck that the King would reach London first. In the end, something of a compromise was reached, whereby the Royalists would stand and fight, taking up a position on the brow of Edgehill. Thus, the morning of 23 October dawned with the King, occupying the high ground, awaiting Essex who was hastily marshalling his men into battle order on the plain beneath. By this time, the armies numbered about 14,000 in total. By nightfall, 1,500 would be dead.

The method of deployment of armies was the same as it had been during the Wars of the Roses, two centuries earlier – infantry massed in the centre with cavalry on each wing. Occupying pride of place on the right of the Royalist line was Prince Rupert, with Henry Wilmot on the left. In the middle were the infantry divisions of Henry Wentworth, Richard Fielding, Charles Gerard and – probably to the rear – those of John Belasyse and Sir Nicholas Byron. For the Parliamentarians, Lord Fielding occupied the right wing and Sir James Ramsay the left, with Sir William Balfour behind. The infantry comprised the brigades of Sir John Meldrum, Colonel Charles Essex and, in the rear, Major-General Thomas Ballard.

One wonders who was the most surprised, the Parliamentarians upon seeing the Royalists leave their vantage point, or the Royalists when Essex allowed them to descend to the plain unmolested. One thing is certain: the Parliamentarians were the first to open fire, with volleys ultimately directed towards the King and his easily identifiable entourage. Charles's aides had difficulty in persuading him to withdraw to a safe position, for he fully intended to fight with his army. Eventually, he retired to higher ground, although he still presented a fair target for the guns of his enemies.

The Parliamentarians may have fired the first shots, but the Royalists responded with spectacular cavalry charges. As Prince Rupert advanced on the right, cannon balls flew harmlessly over his horsemen's heads. A musket volley, discharged before the Royalists were within range, similarly did little damage. Gathering momentum, Rupert's cavalry scattered Ramsay's horse, who were mercilessly pursued by the Royalists, who swept on into Kineton, where the Parliamentarian baggage train was plundered.

On the Royalist left, Wilmot enjoyed similar success. He had a more difficult task, advancing over rough ground, hedges and ditches lined with enemy musketeers. Yet, although the Royalist horse again carried all before them, contemptuously brushing aside Fielding's horse, Wilmot was only marginally more successful than Rupert in halting and rallying his men, most of whom also swept on remorselessly into Kineton. At this point, Balfour's horse advanced to occupy the vacuum created by Fielding's departure and drove forward into the left flank of the Royalist infantry, which retreated before him. Balfour then attacked the Royalists' heavy guns before withdrawing to his own lines. In the process, he was fired on by his own side. Regrouping, and in unison with the right wing of the Parliamentarian infantry, he launched a second attack, threatening the safety of the Royal Standard.

The honour of bearing the Royal Standard had been given to Sir Edmund Verney. He wore no armour and it is said that he had had a premonition of his death upon the battlefield. Struck down by Ensign Arthur Young, Verney was grasping the banner so tightly that his hand had to be hacked from his lifeless body. The banner was actually held by the enemy for only a few moments before being rescued by Captain John Smith, who was knighted for his deed the following day. Smith was to meet his own end two years later at the Battle of Cheriton.

The Royalist infantry in the centre had made progress but, without the benefit of cavalry support, they were doomed. In the nick of time, Prince Rupert returned to the field, and although his men and their mounts were exhausted and in no position to renew hostilities, the Parliamentarians failed to recognise it. It was now growing dark and, horse and foot of both armies having fought to a virtual standstill, each side thought it wise to withdraw to its pre-battle position.

After passing a cold, miserable night in the open, both armies were back in position – the Royalists on Edgehill and the Parliamentarians ranged below them. Neither side was keen to renew hostilities. Although Essex had received infantry reinforcements, his cavalry had been badly mauled, and he was probably relieved when the King began a withdrawal to Edgcote. Essex, in turn, moved to Kineton and then to Warwick – his retreat hampered by Prince Rupert who mounted a successful raid on the Parliamentarian rearguard, capturing guns and supplies.

The guns taken by the Royalists were of heavy calibre and proved a valuable addition to the Royalist arsenal. Muskets, pikes and some armour were also acquired, together with some standards and colours. In those early days, as far as the Royalists were concerned, balancing the books in terms of the capture and loss of regimental colours took precedence over the more mundane issue of men and arms. As the years wore on, the position became reversed as they came, more and more, to appreciate the bread and butter issues upon which the survival of their cause depended.

Reliable estimates of casualties at the Battle of Edgehill have been lost in the propaganda war waged by both sides, Parliamentarian pamphleteers, for example, publicising losses of 3,000 Royalists against 300 of their own. Most probably, casualties were relatively light and evenly balanced, with a total of around 1,500 dead. More would have succumbed to wounds, while there were a considerable number of desertions.

Charles could have pressed on to London but, instead of marching on the capital, which Prince Rupert urged him to do, he wasted time in taking Banbury. From there he marched to Oxford which became his headquarters and the alternative capital for the next four years. Despite the decision to regroup at Oxford, Charles could still have reached London ahead of Essex, who displayed no sense of urgency in returning. The King did not leave Oxford until 3 November. When Charles did get under way, Essex, finally stirred into action, outstripped him, reaching London with the remnants of his army on 7 November. Yet, with Charles now progressing towards the capital, Parliament took fright, Pym announcing a willingness to negotiate. In response, Rupert took Brentford, sweeping aside the garrison which Essex had established there and sacking the town.

Then, on the morning of 13 November, just a couple of miles down the road from Brentford at Turnham Green, Charles found his way forward barred by an army 20,000 strong – Edgehill veterans standing shoulder to shoulder with men of the City of London, trained bands and volunteers who had been streaming out of London throughout the night. What has been called the Battle of Turnham Green was really a stand-off. Outnumbered by two to one, Charles could not risk an attack. Neither could the ill-assorted troops facing him. In the afternoon, the Royalists took the decision to withdraw, making their weary way back to Oxford, which they reached on 29 November. The war was not going to be over by Christmas, after all.

1643: Stalemate

The experience I have had of your worth, and the happiness I have enjoyed in your friendship are wounding considerations when I look upon this present distance between us. Certainly, my affections to you are so unchangeable, that hostility itself cannot violate my friendship to your person... We are both upon the stage and must act those parts assigned to us in this tragedy. Let us do it in a way of honour, and without personal animosities, whatever the issue be, I shall never willingly relinquish the dear title of Your most affectionate friend and faithful servant, Wm. Waller.

Letter, dated 6 June 1643, written by Sir William Waller to Sir Ralph Hopton

On 18 January 1643, Sir Ralph Hopton was appointed Commander-in-Chief of the Royalist Western Army. Although Cornwall was strongly pro-Royalist — and remained so — Hopton's army, 1,500 strong, was penned in. When he broke out into Devon, he was challenged by Colonel William Ruthin, operating out of Plymouth. The armies met at Bradock Down, 30 miles to the west of Plymouth, on 19 January. Hopton set up a defensive position at Bradock Church, taking care to conceal his artillery and part of his force. As Ruthin approached, he was stopped in his tracks by a cannonade. Emerging from their cover, the Royalists attacked, taking the enemy entirely by surprise. Ruthin

escaped but over a thousand of his men were captured, leaving
Hopton secure in Cornwall and with time to prepare for
another breakout into Devon – and, with luck, beyond.

Of rather more strategic significance than the landscape of
Cornwall was the Nottinghamshire town of Newark.
Situated on the River Trent and at the crossroads of the Fosse
Way and the Great North Road, it was described as the 'Key
to the North', and was held for the King from 1642 to 1646.
The first Governor, Sir John Henderson, prepared a narrow
ditch and rampart to surround the town and, on 27 February
1643, he came under attack, with the arrival of 6,000 men
and ten heavy guns under the command of Major-General
Ballard. After subjecting the garrison to a heavy barrage,
Ballard attempted to storm the defences, but he was driven
back by an adventurous counter-charge. His men fled in
disorder. Ballard called off the offensive – the first of many
which Newark endured during the next three years – and
retreated the following day.

Throughout the winter and spring of 1642–43, the two
sides continued half-hearted efforts to reach a negotiated
settlement. A formal presentation on behalf of Parliament
was made at the Treaty of Oxford on 1 February. The
obligatory rantings against the evils of Popery were enhanced
with demands that new laws should be framed for the
persecution of Catholics and that the children of Catholics
must be educated 'by Protestants in the Protestant religion'.
The 'raising, drawing together, and arming of great numbers
of Papists, under the command of the Earl of Newcastle' was
roundly condemned, as was the making of 'Lord Herbert of
Raglan, and other known papists, commanders of great
forces'. The King was to disband his armies, 'as we likewise
shall be ready to disband all those forces which we have

raised' (presumably the implication was that Charles should disarm first) and 'delinquents' were to be handed over to Parliament for punishment. The Propositions also included a list of prominent Parliamentarians for appointment to influential government posts. Needless to add, the talks faltered.

On 22 February, the Queen returned, arriving at Bridlington, having been escorted across the North Sea by Dutch warships. The Earl of Newcastle, who led the Royalist war effort in the North of England, had to drop everything and make a dash for the coast to ensure her safety. She spent her first night in a ditch, under fire from Parliament's navy. Among her personal retinue was a contingent of ladies-in-waiting, her pet dog and a dwarf called Jeffrey Hudson. More to the point, she had also brought a thousand Royalist volunteers, arms and ammunition to fill 250 carts and £80,000 in hard cash. Even so, Newcastle was still expected to fork out £3,000 to cover her living expenses.

Among others who came to pay their respects was the Earl of Montrose, who had changed sides. No longer a Covenanter, he wanted to encourage Charles to support a Royalist rising in Scotland. The Queen promised to pass on his message, but the King was destined to show no interest in the Earl's plans until it was too late. Another guest was Captain John Hotham, son of Sir John Hotham, Governor of Hull. The Hothams were also interested in changing sides – for a price. £20,000 was the sum mentioned. At least Hotham assured her that she would be able to travel to York unhindered. Henrietta Maria reached York on 8 March. Here, Sir Hugh Cholmley, who held Scarborough Castle for Parliament, visited her and promised to change sides. It seemed that her presence was paying dividends, and the sequence of events demonstrated her value to the Royalist cause.

In the early months of 1643, there was still much to play for, particularly since not all the English counties were committed. One of those still up for grabs was Cheshire. Sir Thomas Aston, a member of the local gentry, was instructed to secure it for the Royalists. Parliament, in turn, sent Sir William Brereton. The problem for both sides was that few troops could be spared, and each hoped to raise support in Cheshire itself. Brereton got there first, occupying Nantwich on 28 January. When Aston arrived, his attempts to dislodge Brereton failed and he pulled away to regroup. He had hoped to be reinforced, but the Royalists were already overstretched, with the upkeep of their garrison at Chester being given priority over Aston's pleas for more men. It was not until early March that Aston set out for Middlewich, ten miles to the north of Nantwich, which he had selected as a prospective base. He arrived on 11 March, with a respectable force of 1,000 foot and 500 horse. Brereton, too, had experienced difficulties in obtaining reinforcements and decided to advance on Middlewich with his 500 horse and 200 musketeers.

Brereton attacked on the morning of 13 March. He did not see the weakness of his force as too much of a handicap initially because his men would be advancing through the narrow lanes of the small town, compelling Aston to disperse his own troops, thus sacrificing the advantage of numerical superiority. Nevertheless, Aston had ample time to prepare his defences and he should have been able to stem the flow as the Parliamentarians filtered in from the western approaches. And yet, according to contemporary accounts of the fighting,

Brereton managed to gain footholds from which he could not be dislodged.

Towards mid-morning, Parliamentarian reinforcements arrived from Nantwich – some 800 foot and 300 horse – to attack from the south. Aston had men and artillery waiting for them, but the Royalists lacked the stomach for a fight. Some panicked and took to their heels, while the rest retreated into the town. In such situations, it was not uncommon for troops to fall back on the town church and its surrounding churchyard, and Aston tried to rally his men at the church of St Michael and All Angels. Instead of putting up a fight, however, the Royalists retreated into the church and locked the door. Finding himself almost alone, Aston fled, leaving Brereton to enjoy the spoils of victory – several hundred prisoners and a stock of valuable provisions. Aston's small army had been destroyed and although Chester remained staunchly Royalist, his brief to galvanise Royalist resistance in Cheshire had ended in failure.

Not all was doom and gloom for Royalists in the North. The Earl of Derby conducted a particularly vigorous campaign for the King in Lancashire. It was said of him that he had a greater influence over the people of Lancashire than 'any subject in England had in any other quarter of the kingdom'. This may have been because he ordered his tenants to report for duty 'on pain of death', shooting any who did not display sufficient commitment. On 18 March, he assaulted and plundered Lancaster, two days later he took Preston and, on 28 March, attacked Bolton.

In the Midlands, Royalist Lichfield came under threat when it was targeted by Lord Brooke, for Parliament. The short campaign which followed was unlucky for both sides. On 2 March, as he surveyed Lichfield, Brooke was shot dead by a sniper. Nevertheless, the town was taken and garrisoned, owing to the efforts of Sir John Gell of Hopton. Intent on reversing the situation, a Royalist army under Sir Henry Hastings and the Earl of Northampton was soon on the move, reaching Stafford on 18 March.

Gell marched out from Lichfield, having arranged to meet Sir William Brereton on Hopton Heath, three miles to the north of Stafford. Gell arrived at the rendezvous on the morning of Sunday 19 March, deploying his infantry on high ground, with dragoons on their left flank. Brereton and his own dragoons arrived in the early afternoon – his infantry was trailing behind – and positioned them on the right flank. Hastings and Northampton were caught unawares and hurriedly marshalled their forces. As soon as they arrived on the heath, at about 3 o'clock in the afternoon, they went on to the attack. The dragoons on both Parliamentarian flanks were driven from their vantage points, and Northampton charged Gell's infantry. Driven back by determined resistance, he led a second charge, but was unhorsed. Surrounded by the enemy, he died fighting on foot. Try what they may, the Royalists could not break the determined resistance of Gell's infantry. When Gell was reinforced by the timely arrival of Brereton's infantry, the Royalists drew off. During the night Gell retired to Uttoxeter. The Royalists had, for the moment, saved Stafford – and captured a number of cannon – but at the cost of Northampton's life. Gell took the body away, offering to exchange it for the captured cannon. When the offer was turned down, Gell had the Earl's body stripped, thrown over a horse and put on public display.

In the North, the Royalist Earl of Newcastle's task was a monumental one. He was immensely wealthy but, although the fighting focused largely on Yorkshire, he had responsibility for all the land from the Scottish borders to the River Humber. Pitted against him were Lord Fairfax and his son, Sir Thomas. Both had seen service abroad, but they were unable to match the resources Newcastle had at his disposal, and were continuously on the back foot, Newcastle actively pursuing them throughout the Ridings. Towards the end of March, they were withdrawing westwards from Selby to Leeds, with Newcastle intent on intercepting them. Sir Thomas made a diversionary attack on Royalist Tadcaster in an attempt to cover Lord Fairfax's march. He drove out the defenders, which succeeded in bringing Newcastle to a halt. Having gained some four hours, Sir Thomas pulled out. As he did so, George Goring and twenty troops of cavalry and dragoons arrived.

Goring gave chase and Fairfax used his three troops of horse to cover the retreat of his infantry over Bramham Moor. The infantry's progress was painfully slow and he formed them up in good marching order, Goring following 'about two musket shot from us'. They were still some five miles from Leeds when they approached Seacroft Moor — like Bramham Moor, an open plain. Here, they paused, entering houses in search of water, for it was an 'exceedingly hot' day. By the time they had been mustered, Goring was upon them, Sir Thomas reporting that the Royalists attacked to both flank and rear, putting his infantry to flight. 'Some were slain; and many taken prisoners'. The cavalry also failed to withstand the assault and Sir Thomas, in company with a handful of officers, struggled in to Leeds about two hours after the arrival of Lord Fairfax. The objective of covering the retreat of the main force had been achieved, and the running fight scarcely rates a mention in military histories, but Sir Thomas himself described it as 'one of the greatest losses we ever received'.

Back in Cornwall, the sparring between Royalists and Parliamentarians continued. On 25 April, Hopton allowed himself to be ambushed at Sourton Down, near Okehampton, falling victim to much the same kind of trickery he himself had employed when he had engineered the ambush of Ruthin at Bradock Down in January. His force was badly shaken and his personal papers were taken, including a letter from the King ordering him to join the Earl of Hertford and Prince Maurice. The Earl of Stamford, Parliamentarian commander in Devon, knew he had to stop the planned link-up and moved his army – 5,500 strong – to Stratton, near Bude, deploying his men on an iron-age hill fort, known ever since as Stamford Hill. Hopton, heavily outnumbered, approached the position on 15 May. The eastern slope of the hill was very steep and the Parliamentarians had their backs to it. Hopton divided his infantry into four columns consisting of 600 men each and, at dawn on 16 May, launched an assault on the three open sides. The Royalist advance was dogged but, by 3 o'clock in the afternoon, they had failed to reach the hilltop. They were also running out of ammunition for their artillery and, had the Parliamentarians stayed put, Hopton would have had to withdraw.

Unexpectedly, however, Major-General James Chudleigh chose this moment to lead his infantrymen downhill, to attack the column led by Sir Bevil Grenville, which wilted under the assault. Grenville himself was 'overthrown'. A Royalist counter-charge from Sir John Berkeley steadied the line, throwing back Chudleigh's men, and Chudleigh himself was taken prisoner. Redoubling their efforts, the Royalists pressed onwards and upwards, reaching the top of the hill by 4 o'clock, at which juncture the defenders gave up the fight. Some managed to escape and Stamford himself sought the protection afforded by Parliamentarian Exeter, but 1,700 of his men were captured and his army effectively destroyed.

*

Throughout England, it seemed, the morale of the King's armies was prevailing against the superior strength of the Parliamentarians. Another instance of the triumph of mind over matter was provided, fittingly, by Prince Rupert. While quartered at Oxford, he was approached by John Hurry, a professional turncoat. The artful Hurry brought the tempting intelligence that the Parliamentarian paymaster, in charge of a sum in excess of £20,000, was en route to Thame to pay the troops. Rupert's response was characteristically bold. Giving but little consideration to Hurry's doubtful references, he resolved to intercept and appropriate the Parliamentarian pay packets.

On 17 June, Rupert left the Royalist capital, accompanied by 1,800 men. Early the next day, he reached Postcombe, a hamlet near Chinnor, where he trounced a troop of Parliamentarian horse. Quickly advancing to Chinnor itself, the Royalists surprised the garrison, killing or capturing nearly two hundred dragoons. The exercise, although a splendid example of the cut and thrust guerrilla tactics in which Rupert excelled, failed in its objective, for the paymaster's convoy responded to the alarums and excursions by running for cover.

Having failed in his mission, and knowing that the Parliamentarians were aware of his location, Rupert had to engineer a withdrawal to the safety of Oxford. The main route, via Thame, he knew would be barred and so he swept south, to Chiselhampton. Progress was slow. His men had been on the move since the previous afternoon and had seen action twice – and by mid-morning, skirmishes with parties of the enemy horse were occurring. At about 9 o'clock, Rupert halted in a field near the village of Chalgrove, three miles from the Chiselhampton crossing of the River Thame. Dragoons and infantry were sent forward to secure the bridge, while the cavalry remained drawn up under cover of a hedge. The Prince was urged to press on, but he was able to see that disaster could result if his men came under fire while they were crossing the river. While the Royalists deliberated, eight troops of Parliamentarian dragoons appeared on the other side of the hedge.

In true Cavalier fashion, Rupert spurred on his horse and cleared the hedge, closely followed by his Life Guard – a number of whom were picked off by the waiting dragoons. The remainder of the Royalist horse, in more conventional fashion, rode around the hedge to join the mêlée. To their credit, Stapleton's main body of horse tried to make a fight of it but, being outnumbered, they were soon outflanked and routed. Rupert was able to march on to Chiselhampton to cross the river in safety. At 2 o'clock in the afternoon, he entered Oxford in triumph with one hundred prisoners and a selection of pennants and colours – but not, as his critics remarked wryly, the £20,000 he had set out to capture.

The Royalists attached great importance to the battle, which had been little more than a skirmish. In one respect, however, it had been significant, for it resulted in the death of John Hampden. Having risen from his bed, he had attached himself to Stapleton's command and, in the thick of the fighting, he was mortally wounded, either by enemy musket fire or by the misfiring of his own pistol. A week later, despite the King's gallant offer to send his personal physician to attend upon him, he died.

*

In the North, the Earl of Newcastle was unstoppable. He hoped to put an end to the Fairfaxes by taking Bradford, their major base. On 22 June, he captured Rowley House, a Parliamentarian stronghold between Leeds and Wakefield. Then, on the morning of 30 June, with some 9,000 men, he set out for Bradford. Having little hope of mounting a credible defence, the Fairfaxes decided to march out to meet Newcastle, with the aim of surprising him. They had intended to start out no later than 4 o'clock on the morning of 30 June, but did not get underway much before 8 o'clock. In fact, they had marched but four miles when they came upon the Royalists, ready and waiting for them on a plain by the village of Adwalton.

Lord Fairfax, leading an ill-assorted crew of horse and foot, was outnumbered by three to one. He deployed his men in traditional battalia, Major-General John Gifford on the left and Sir Thomas on the right, with his infantry in the centre. His mobility was compromised by a number of enclosures and, although Newcastle's three divisions were deployed over open ground, the Royalist left-wing was somewhat hampered by open-cast coalmines. Fairfax did possess one advantage in that he had twice as many musketeers as Newcastle – all experienced men who were put to good use behind the hedgerows that defined the enclosures.

Almost at once, Newcastle put Sir Thomas under pressure, unleashing '10 or 12 Troops of horse' against him. By utilising the cover afforded by the enclosures, however, Sir Thomas withstood the attack. A second charge was not quite so easily dealt with, 'many having got in among us', but Sir Thomas regrouped, counter-attacked and pursued the enemy back to their own lines. According to Sir Thomas, the Parliamentarian left wing was obscured by a ridge, making it difficult to know how Gifford was faring. He had been making ground when a charge by Royalist infantry bore fruit. Led by a Colonel Skirton, described by Sir Thomas as 'a wild and desperate man', the assault sent Gifford's men reeling. Having broken Gifford's line, the Royalists were able to sweep around to the rear of the Parliamentarian centre. As soon as he realised he had been outflanked, Lord Fairfax ordered a general retreat. Caught up in a relentless pursuit, he headed for Bradford, while his son fled to Halifax.

Newcastle claimed that 500 Parliamentarians were killed and 1,400 taken prisoner, while his own casualties – if he is to be believed – were remarkably light, amounting to only 22 dead. Despite the unequal nature of the contest, Newcastle was honoured by being created Marquess of Newcastle. Now nearly all Yorkshire – with the very notable exception of Hull – lay at his feet.

At least it would now be safe to despatch Henrietta Maria to Oxford. Apprised of her approach, Charles rode out to meet her and, on 13 July, they were reunited on the field of Edgehill. The next night, they entered Oxford where the Queen was received with much ceremony. She remained there for nine months, during which time the social gaieties in the new Royalist capital reached their zenith.

*

Earlier in the year, Parliament had appointed Sir William Waller commander of its forces in the West, which meant that, sooner or later, he would be pitted against Sir Ralph Hopton. The two men were friends, having served together in the Thirty Years War in the 1620s, and theirs is one of the great human stories of the Civil War. Although they fought for their chosen cause – often against one another – they kept up a regular and friendly correspondence throughout.

In the aftermath of Stratton, Hertford had managed to join forces with Hopton to create a combined force of 4,000 foot, 2,000 cavalry and 300 dragoons. Meanwhile, Waller was unable to scrape together so many men, and was particularly short of cavalry, although he did acquire the services of Sir Arthur Haselrig. Eccentric, yet bold in battle, Sir Arthur became a fixture in Waller's army. He had assembled his own regiment of cuirassiers, nicknamed 'Lobsters' because of their full body armour, which rendered them virtually impervious to injury in the normal course of combat.

The two armies met on 5 July at Lansdown Hill, to the north of Bath, Waller having occupied the northern portion of the hill, upon which he constructed breastworks as cover for his infantry. Concealed in woodland on both flanks were musketeers. Hopton, meanwhile, was assembling his army on Tog Hill, one and a half miles to the north-east. Such fighting as occurred during the day was confined to skirmishes between the opposing parties of dragoons, notably in the area of Freezing Hill, mid-way between the two positions. By the afternoon, the Royalist dragoons had been pushed back to the foot of Tog Hill, and a shortage of ammunition – not an unusual occurrence for the Royalists – led to Hopton's withdrawal towards nearby Marshfield.

At this juncture, Waller made a bold decision and sent a force of around 800 men – cavalry and dragoons – to attack the retreating Royalists. Initially, the tactic bore fruit, the Royalist horse recoiling upon their own infantry. The situation was redeemed by units of Cornish musketeers, deployed on the orders of Prince Maurice, who held their ground until the Earl of Carnarvon's Regiment of Horse was able to counter-attack. Despite sustaining a wound in the action, Carnarvon managed to turn the Parliamentarians, who began to fall back towards their own lines. Hopton decided to go over onto the offensive. Regrouping, Royalist horse and foot began a steady advance on Waller's centre, while flanking parties of musketeers advanced in woodland to left and right. Soon, Sir Bevil Grenville's regiment, leading the advance, was making its way, under heavy fire, up the hill. The cover afforded by hedges and walls meant that their casualties were light, but when they reached the brow of the hill, their lines were raked by case-shot and musket-volleys. Even so, a number of Parliamentarian charges led by Haselrig and Waller himself failed to blunt the assault, although Grenville was killed.

A particularly graphic account of the action was provided by Royalist captain, Richard Atkyns. 'The air was so darkened by the smoke of the powder,' he says, 'that for a quarter of an hour together there was no light seen, but what the fire of the volleys of shot gave; and 'twas the greatest storm that ever I saw...' He adds that Grenville's infantry, though deprived of their leader, was magnificent, standing 'as upon the eaves of an house for steepness, but as unmovable as a rock'.

As the battle wore on through the late afternoon and into the early evening, Hopton's numerical advantage began to tell. After some heavy fighting in the woods, the Royalist musketeers broke through on both flanks, and light artillery was brought up, forcing Waller to abandon his breastworks. A sheepcote surrounded by a high stone wall lay to the rear, and the Parliamentarians took cover behind it. The fighting subsided into a medium-range musketry duel in which the Royalists, struggling to consolidate their position on the brow of the hill, were at a disadvantage. The onset of darkness saved them from severe punishment, although they were kept pinned down in the hollows, where they had sought shelter, throughout the evening.

Both sides went in fear of a night attack for, as was customary in such stand-off situations, each thought they had lost. At about 1 o'clock in the morning, Maurice discerned that Waller was on the move. An unexpected volley of musket fire suggested that the Parliamentarians were, indeed, about to attack. After an hour, however, all was quiet and Waller was found to have withdrawn towards Bath, leaving lit matches along the top of the stone wall and pikes standing upright, so as to give the impression that his defences were still manned.

Royalist casualties had been heavy, but Hopton was able to claim the victory. At length, he retired to Tog Hill where some enemy prisoners had been placed in an ammunition cart containing several barrels of gunpowder. As Hopton passed by, one of the prisoners accidentally dropped a match among the barrels. The resulting explosion, which could be heard in Bath, left Hopton temporarily blinded and paralysed. Nevertheless, his army was shortly on the march, arriving at Devizes on 9 July. Having regrouped, Waller was soon in pursuit, taking up a position on Roundway Hill, two miles to the north of the town.

On the evening of 10 July, it was decided that Hopton, still seriously incapacitated, would remain in Devizes with the infantry, while Hertford and Maurice made the 40-mile journey to Oxford in order to acquire reinforcements. At midnight, the cavalry duly broke out, unchallenged. For the next three days, Waller subjected Devizes to a continuous artillery barrage. Then, on 13 July, he learned of the approach, from Marlborough, of a Royalist relief force. Hastily assembled, it consisted of three brigades commanded by Lord Wilmot, Sir John Byron and the Earl of Crawford – and yet Waller, with some 2,000 horse and 2,500 foot, still enjoyed a measure of numerical superiority. Waller deployed his army between Roundway Hill and King's Play Hill, his infantry in the centre flanked by cavalry commanded by Haselrig on the right and Waller himself on the left.

It had been part of the Royalist plan for Hopton's infantry to attack the Parliamentarian rear but Hopton failed to move. Wilmot, the senior Royalist commander on the spot, decided to attack regardless. An advance guard, dispatched by Waller to harass the advancing Royalist horse, was swept aside. Sir Arthur Haselrig, probably on his own authority, led his cuirassiers forward but they too were forced to quit the field. The encounter between Waller and Sir John Byron that followed forced Waller back onto his own reserves. Running for their lives, many Parliamentarians came to grief during their rapid descent of a concealed steep escarpment. Rallying his horse, Wilmot tried to break the enemy infantry which, under Waller's personal direction, withstood a number of charges. Only when Hopton's infantry made a belated appearance, marching out from Devizes, did Waller withdraw. Left to fend for themselves, his infantrymen were picked off by Wilmot's pursuing cavalry.

Waller had lost the battle, his army and, as far as his critics were concerned, his credibility. In a little over a week, he had transformed a threatening situation into a promising one, only to have the final victory, in what should have been his finest hour, torn cruelly from his grasp. The destruction of Waller's army opened the road to Bristol. The third city in the kingdom, it was a thriving manufacturing centre and a busy seaport, through which might flow fresh supplies of men and materials to feed the Royalist war machine – if it could be freed from Parliamentarian control.

Hertford, Hopton and Maurice were joined by Prince Rupert from Oxford and, on 23 July, their massed armies assembled before the city, the defences of which were formidable. An outer ring consisted of a wall punctuated at intervals by a number of forts and batteries. An inner ring protecting the city centre was formed largely by the Rivers Avon and Frome. Against this was set the fact that Waller had drawn out over 1,000 men to fight at Roundway Down, leaving Nathaniel Fiennes, the Parliamentarian governor of the city, in command of a garrison of only 1,200 foot and 300 horse.

At 11 o'clock on the morning of 24 July, Rupert invited Fiennes to surrender. When he refused, the Royalists deployed their artillery and discussed possible strategies. The Western Army had envisaged a regular siege, but Rupert insisted upon attacking. The idea was to co-ordinate an assault on the north and south sides of the city, but the Cornishmen attacked early, at about 3 o'clock on the morning of 26 July. Their task was the harder, for they faced the toughest defences and they suffered heavy casualties. On the north side, the defences were not so stout and Fiennes had to spread his forces thinly. After some heavy fighting, Rupert broke through, the defenders retreating towards the city centre. Fiennes capitulated.

The terms of surrender allowed for the garrison's officers to depart in possession of their horses and swords, but the weaponry of the infantry, together with artillery and all ammunition had to be handed over. When the Parliament-arians marched out the next day, however, everything did not go smoothly, for 'some were plundered out of the town'. According to Fiennes, Rupert and Maurice discouraged such behaviour by riding 'among the plunderers with their swords, hacking and slashing them'.

The capture of Bristol was also marred by Rupert's deficiency in tact. Hertford complained that Maurice had been acting without consulting him and Rupert exacerbated the issue by requesting his own appointment as Governor. Hertford responded by announcing that the job was going to Hopton. Charles should have overruled Rupert but, blood being thicker than water, he rode over to Bristol to confirm his nephew's appointment. In turn, Rupert offered Hopton the post of his second-in-command, promising that he 'would not at all meddle in the government' of the city. Maurice was promoted to the rank of general, Hopton was given a peerage, and Hertford accompanied Charles back to Oxford.

*

In the North, the Fairfaxes were still under pressure, for Newcastle had them boxed in at Bradford — Sir Thomas reporting that his father was 'much troubled; having neither a place of strength to defend ourselves in, nor a garrison in Yorkshire to retreat to'. On 30 June, Lord Fairfax broke out and made for Leeds, which he hoped to secure, while Sir Thomas kept the Royalists occupied. In the early hours of 2 July, after repelling a number of punishing assaults, Sir Thomas was reduced to one barrel of gunpowder and no matches for his muskets. Accordingly, he decided to join his father. With difficulty, he got through, losing many of his men – and his wife, who was captured – in the process. Instead of finding a safe haven at Leeds, he discovered 'all in great distraction'. Now in headlong retreat, father and son, with a mere handful of troops, moved on to Selby. Following a running fight, during the course of which Sir Thomas was wounded in the wrist, they crossed the River Ouse, reaching Hull, only after a 'very troublesome and dangerous passage'.

There was now grave concern in Parliament over the prospect of Newcastle marching south. Nothing, it seemed, could stand in his way. On 20 July, a glimmer of hope was provided by Lord Willoughby, the Parliamentarian commander in Lincolnshire, who occupied Gainsborough. It remained to be seen whether he could hold on to it, for Newcastle sent his young cousin, Sir Charles Cavendish, with a strong body of horse, to challenge him. Sir John Meldrum marched from Nottingham to lend Willoughby support. At Grantham, he was joined by Cromwell who had been engaged in clearing Royalist troops from Stamford and Burghley House. Cavendish was awaiting their arrival, his men deployed on a plateau to the north-east of the town.

The exact sequence of events is uncertain, but the Parliamentarians made their way up to the plateau and charged the Royalists. 'We came up horse to horse,' says Cromwell, 'where we disputed it with our swords and pistols a pretty time... At last, they a little shrinking, our men, perceiving it, pressed in upon them, and immediately routed the whole body.' However, the wily Cavendish placed himself at the head of a regiment he had held in reserve, intending to charge the victorious but unsuspecting Parliamentarians as they pursued their fleeing quarry. Cromwell spotted the trap and, rallying his own troops, attacked from behind.

Cavendish and his men were driven headlong down the hill. Cavendish himself was unhorsed and stabbed to death by a Parliamentarian officer as he lay helpless.

Soon afterwards, news arrived that a modest Royalist force was approaching from the north. Meldrum and Cromwell gathered together some 400 foot and went to meet it – and came face to face with Newcastle's main army. There was no panic, and they made a fighting withdrawal, alternately retiring and facing the enemy. Although Gainsborough soon fell to Newcastle and Willoughby's army melted away, the Battle of Gainsborough has been called the turning point of the war, supplying proof that the Parliamentarians could field a disciplined body of horse, tactically capable of punishing the enemy.

Another sign that the tide was about to turn occurred at Parliamentarian Gloucester, with the arrival of the King's army and an invitation, made on 10 August, for the garrison to surrender. A Royal pardon was promised to all the inhabitants, with a rider to the effect that, should they refuse this generous offer, they must be prepared to suffer the consequences. A carefully worded reply assured the King that his dutiful subjects would hold Gloucester for him, obeying his commands as 'signified by both Houses of Parliament'.

Those same Houses of Parliament despatched a relief column, led by the Earl of Essex, towards Gloucester. It left London on 26 August, but its progress was painfully slow, sometimes consisting of as little as three and a half miles in a day. As Essex finally approached Gloucester, the Royalists sneakily spread a rumour to the effect that his army had been engaged and destroyed, but the garrison refused to bite. Then, on 5 September, the besiegers were observed destroying their camp and retreating to the south. Charles had realised that his plans had gone awry and, not wishing to risk his cavalry in broken country, had taken the decision to withdraw, allowing Essex (who arrived on 8 September) to claim an easy victory.

In fact, the King was in better shape than Essex. The Royalists had stripped the surrounding countryside and the Parliamentarians crowded into the town to forage for food. Charles could either get between Essex's poorly provisioned troops and London, and bring him to battle, or he could try to reach the capital first. He must have been mindful of the shambles at Turnham Green and, ideally, he needed to destroy Essex's army *and* reach the capital.

*

Behind the scenes, both sides were engaged in plans to increase their fighting strength. The Royalists concentrated on Ireland where Charles, working through Ormonde, achieved the 'Irish Cessation', a temporary truce with O'Neill's rebels which facilitated the return of English troops to fight for the Royalist cause on home ground. Parliament had been pushing for a military alliance with the Scots. This came to fruition in September as 'The Solemn League and Covenant'. It stopped short of an agreement to introduce Presbyterianism into England, with an undertaking to 'bring the Churches of God in the three kingdoms [England, Ireland and Scotland] to the nearest conjunction and uniformity in religion, confession of faith, form of Church government… that we, and our posterity after us, may, as brethren, live in faith and love, and the Lord may delight to dwell in the midst of us'. Given an additional sweetener of £30,000 per month, the Scots agreed to send an army into England.

*

On 29 June 1643, the Parliamentarian garrison at Hull had quashed the Hothams' plot to hand over the city to the Royalists. Sir John Hotham was arrested and Lord Fairfax appointed in his place. Hull's defences were formidable. To the south lay the River Humber and to the east, the River Hull (with a fort, 'South End', built in 1627) and, beyond that, a fortified wall which included a castle and two blockhouses. To the north and west was a moat, surmounted by four fortified gateways: Hessle Gate, Myton Gate, North Gate and Beverley Gate. It was very unlikely that it would ever be taken by force, but Newcastle, reluctant to proceed further south until Hull had been secured, turned back to address the problem.

He began siege operations in the early hours of 2 September, eventually constructing a series of earthworks to the north and east of the city. One line stretched north along the road to Beverley; a second line hugged the west bank of the River Hull and a third, beginning at a point known as 'The Gallows' and only 500 metres from the city wall, was strung out to the west. Meanwhile, the garrison managed to construct earthworks of its own outside the walls – 'Mount Fort' beneath Hessle Gate, to protect the West Jetty, and a second beyond North Gate. It was common practice for the besieged to use women for this work. It may have been perceived as a woman's job, but it is more likely that it was hoped the enemy would think twice before opening fire on them. And Newcastle was a chivalrous opponent, for he released Sir Thomas's wife from her captivity and sent her to join him.

There were, however, limits to Newcastle's generosity, and he commandeered all foodstuffs from the surrounding countryside and cut off the fresh water supply. In response, Lord Fairfax ordered the Humber's banks to be cut, flooding the land for two miles around. The countryside to the east was particularly badly affected, resulting in little military activity, but heavy rains and high tides ensured that the besiegers on all sides endured miserable conditions. Fortunately for the garrison, the back door was kept open by two of Parliament's warships, *Rainbow* and *Unicorn*, which retained control of the River Humber, guaranteeing supplies. Sir Thomas Fairfax was even able to take 20 troops of cavalry over to Lincolnshire to join the Earl of Manchester.

The defenders were also able to launch their own sorties outside the walls. On 11 October, 1,000 musketeers made a three-pronged assault on the earthwork known as 'The Gallows'. The Royalists were driven back, first from 'The Gallows' and then from a second entrenchment, but reinforcements were brought up, enabling them to regain some ground. In a bold move, however, Lord Fairfax refused to allow his men back into the city. Thus encouraged, they renewed their attack, recapturing the Royalist positions. When they did eventually withdraw, they did so with several pieces of Royalist artillery. In a last-ditch effort to make an impression, Newcastle launched an all-out attack, committing 4,000 troops to an assault on the West Jetty. They came within a pistol-shot of attaining their objective when a counter-attack compelled them to retreat.

*

In fact, in what had hitherto been a relatively low-key theatre of operations in the East, the Royalists were generally feeling the pinch in terms of a shortage of manpower. The decision was taken to pare down to a bare minimum the strength of garrisons not under immediate threat. By creaming off troops from Newark, Lincoln and Gainsborough, a 2,500 strong force was assembled in order to meet the threat posed by the Earl of Manchester's Army of the Eastern Association. Initially designed to defend the counties of Norfolk, Suffolk, Essex, Cambridgeshire and Huntingdonshire – and with Cromwell serving as a colonel of cavalry – the army was now moving further afield.

On 9 October, Manchester laid siege to Bolingbroke, taking the precaution of sending Fairfax to do some prospecting around Horncastle to the north. On 10 October, Fairfax encountered the Royalist task force, commanded by Sir William Widdrington and Sir John Henderson. There was little he could do to halt the advance, but he could slow it down by skirmishing while conducting an orderly retreat towards Manchester's main army which was now marching from Bolingbroke towards Horncastle, on a route which would take it through Winceby. Less than a mile beyond that hamlet, the Royalists, who marginally outnumbered Manchester's men, were drawing up in battle order.

Manchester was keen on forcing a confrontation, although Cromwell was against it. Both armies occupied ridges about half a mile apart. In the middle was open ground, dipping slightly – the preferred setting for Civil War battles since it favoured the movement of cavalry. Manchester organised a vanguard comprising his own regiment and that of Cromwell, supported by Fairfax in the rear. In front was a company of dragoons, commanded by Colonel Bartholomew Vermuyden. The foot, led by Sir Miles Hobart, had not yet arrived and Manchester went off to chase them up. The Royalist vanguard, composed of dragoons, was supported by three divisions of cavalry, with Henderson on the left, Sir William Savile on the right and Widdrington in the rear. Neither Widdrington nor Manchester, it would appear, intended to lead from the front.

Battle commenced with the advance of the Royalist vanguard. Vermuyden responded, both sides dismounting and opening fire. As Royalist and Parliamentarian cavalry began to move down the slope from either ridge, Cromwell's horse was shot from under him. Rising to his feet, he was knocked down by a Royalist, Sir Ingram Hopton. Had Hopton chosen to despatch Cromwell there and then, history would have been very different. Probably acting out of a sense of honour, he took Cromwell prisoner instead. In the confusion following the clash of cavalry, however, Hopton was killed and a Parliamentarian trooper provided Cromwell with a replacement mount. At this point, accounts of the battle become diversified. According to the popular version, Cromwell remounted, rallied the troops and led a second charge which put the opposition to flight. This is unlikely, as he would have needed time to familiarise himself with his new mount. There was, indeed, a decisive Parliamentarian assault but it was led by Fairfax, who moved up onto the ridge to the right and attacked diagonally across the hollow, breaking Savile's horse. As was so often the case, the collapse of one wing led to a rout.

Despite the weariness of their mounts, the Parliamentarians pressed home their advantage, Savile's men being driven back off the road and into the fields. They were halted in their flight by a high hedge. The good news that the hedge was broken by a gate quickly turned into bad news when it was discovered that the gate opened inwards, towards the mass of horsemen. Unable to escape, the Royalists were cut to pieces – the spot acquiring the graphic title 'Slash Hollow'. The dismounted dragoons were slaughtered where they stood. Henderson and Widdrington had a more open line of retreat, but they fared badly, many Royalists falling to the east of Winceby, in Snipe Dale. The fighting had been short and sharp and was over before the arrival of Hobart's infantry, which was sufficiently fresh to join in the pursuit for several miles. The surviving Royalists fell back on Lincoln while the victorious Parliamentarians settled for a well-earned night's rest in Horncastle.

When he learned of the Royalist defeat at Winceby, Newcastle decided to call it a day. Winter was approaching and Hull had absorbed everything he could throw at it. He cut his losses by lifting the siege and withdrawing towards York, allowing the citizens of Hull to emerge from their confinement to level all the earthworks. This, rather than Gainsborough, was surely *the* turning point in the war. Instead of marching on London, Newcastle's army had been tied down for six weeks, buying Parliament valuable time to strengthen its position in Lincolnshire and beyond.

During the course of hostilities, both sides expended considerable time and resources in conducting sieges, which constituted a third of all military actions and resulted in about 25% of the war's total death toll. Many, like the Siege of Gloucester, were pointless and succeeded only in tying up armies which would have been better employed elsewhere. As he retreated from Gloucester, Charles had been particularly disconsolate. When asked by the young Duke of York whether they were now going home, he uttered his famous response: 'We have no home.'

*

After relieving Gloucester, Essex had needed time to rest

and provision his troops, and it was not until 15 September that he finally turned for London. However, the King, too, had loitered and, at first, Essex kept marginally ahead. Thanks to the successful harrying of Essex's column by Prince Rupert, however, the Royalists were able to gain the advantage, reaching Newbury on 19 September. When Essex appeared, late in the day, he found the King's army occupying a position to the west of the town. To his surprise, he also discovered that the Royalists had failed to take possession of the one topographical feature which would prove to be of vital importance in any battle – the high ground known as Round Hill.

Early on the morning of 20 September, Essex deployed his men across Wash Common, to the west of the Royalists. His left wing comprised infantry (Major Richard Fortesque and Lord Robartes) and cavalry (Colonel John Middleton). The right wing comprised cavalry (Sir Philip Stapleton), with infantry (Essex and Philip Skippon) in the centre, manoeuvring into position on Round Hill. The Royalists now had to take Round Hill, which was clearly the key to the battle and which could have been occupied with ease the night before. The Royalist left wing comprised the cavalry of Prince Rupert and Colonel Charles Gerrard. Infantry commanded by Sir William Vavasour occupied the right. In the centre was the infantry of Sir Nicholas Byron, with the cavalry of Sir John Byron and Sir Arthur Aston. The battle opened with an assault by Sir Nicholas and Sir John Byron (uncle and nephew respectively) on Round Hill. The defenders were well placed but, despite suffering heavy casualties, the Byrons managed to establish a tenuous foothold on the north-east corner.

Contemporary accounts of the action on the

Parliamentarian left are scant, but it is known that Fortesque did come under intense pressure from Vavasour. With the baggage train to his rear, it was essential for Fortesque to hold on and he was reinforced by Sir William Springate's regiment. On the Parliamentarian right, over terrain more suitable for cavalry than the centre, Rupert made a series of assaults on Stapleton. At the third attempt, Stapleton was forced to give ground. When he did so, Rupert overplayed his hand (as usual, one is bound to say) by pushing too far forward, and was ambushed by Parliamentarian dragoons. Essex was to be seen within Stapleton's broken lines, trying to stabilise them.

This was one of the few battles in the Civil War in which artillery played a major role, and Skippon brought more guns forward, along with reserves. Although the Royalist guns inflicted heavy damage, the Parliamentarian cannon also wrought considerable havoc among the Royalist horse and foot. The barrage went on throughout the day, but neither side was able to deliver a knockout blow. When the fighting drew to a close towards 7 o'clock in the evening, Essex thought (as he had at Edgehill) that the battle would be resumed upon the morrow. The main problem for the Royalists, however, was the fact that they were running short of ammunition. Only ten barrels of powder remained from the ninety barrels with which they had started the day. There was nothing for it but to withdraw, and it came as a welcome surprise to Essex the following dawn to find the Royalists gone and the road to the capital open.

Casualties had been heavy. About 3,500 men had lost their lives and one Royalist officer witnessed, 'A whole file of men, six deep, with their heads struck off with one cannon shot'. Both commanders were solicitous about the care of the dead and wounded, Essex instructing local parish constables to attend to the burial of all corpses, while the King ordered the Mayor of Newbury to ensure that wounded Parliamentarians were given the same degree of medical attention as the Royalists. As it was standard practice for the victorious general to give permission for enemy wounded to be carried away, perhaps both used the custom as a means of claiming victory. In retrospect, however, the Parliamentarians must be regarded as the winners, if only because Essex had achieved his purpose of raising the Siege of Gloucester and returning to London. All Charles could do was withdraw once more to Oxford.

In rather better spirits and commanding a new Western army of 3,000 foot and 1,500 horse – partially made up of regiments returning from Ireland – Lord Hopton was on the march eastwards. He secured Winchester, establishing garrisons at Romsey and Alton, but was unable to advance further than Arundel, having been stopped in his tracks by Parliamentarian resistance at Bramber. This reverse was unexpected, and Hopton's army was strung out almost thirty miles along the Alton-Arundel road.

On the evening of 12 December, Hopton's old friend Sir William Waller, was at Farnham. He devised a cunning plan to take Alton, setting out after midnight and avoiding the main roads. Famous for his night marches, he had acquired the nickname of 'The Night Owl' and perhaps Hopton should have anticipated the strategy. The Earl of Crawford, commanding Alton's Royalist garrison, had posted sentries on the northern approaches and the alarm was raised before dawn. According to Parliamentarian accounts, Crawford fled to Winchester with his cavalry; the Royalist version has him going to Winchester with the aim of returning with reinforcements. Whatever the justification, the infantry, commanded by Colonel Richard Boles, were left to mount a defence.

Boles concentrated his men on rising ground centred on St Lawrence's church and a number of stone houses and barns. As Waller made his way towards the churchyard, a fierce firefight developed between the musketeers of both sides. Gradually, the defenders were pushed back into the church itself, where the fighting continued – Boles, it was said, directing resistance from the pulpit until he fell. After his death, his men surrendered – some 900 were gathered in – and marched off in captivity to Farnham.

This was not the end of the 1643 fighting season for, on Christmas Eve, there occurred one of the most notorious massacres of the Civil War. It took place in St Bertoline's church in the village of Barthomley, Cheshire. Twenty parishioners had taken refuge in the church, retreating into the steeple when Royalists, led by Major John Connaught, broke in. Connaught set fire to the church furniture and smoked them out. It was subsequently claimed that they had asked for and had been given quarter but, once he had them in his grasp, Connaught had them slaughtered. According to the Royalists, the parishioners were, in fact, rebels who had refused to surrender. Whatever the truth of the matter, it was a propaganda coup for Parliament. Connaught himself was brought to book at Chester Assizes in 1654, when he was hanged for personally cleaving the skull of one of the captives with a battle axe.

One of the most momentous events of the year – possibly *the* most momentous for Parliament – had occurred on 8 December, when John Pym died. His last act was to manoeuvre the Solemn League and Covenant through

Parliament, but he had also been responsible for organising the framework of taxation to finance the Parliamentarian war effort. There was no one to replace him and, had he lived, one wonders how he would have managed the future conflict between Parliament and the New Model Army – and, indeed, whether Cromwell's subsequent rise to power would have materialised.

1644: The Queen Withdraws

*My Dear Heart, I know when you hear of our great battle with
Prince Rupert you will be very fearful of me; therefore I write to satisfy
thee that God hath also, at this time, preserved me from any hurt at
all... I cannot stay the messenger, so you must excuse me to all my
friends, and tell them I had not any paper but this, and it was a piece
of a letter... so I rest thy dear husband, Will Fairfax.*

Letter from Sir William Fairfax written to his wife in the
aftermath of Marston Moor. Sir William was killed in action
later in the year

The year 1644 began well for Parliament. On 19 January, the
Scots arrived, with the Earl of Leven leading 20 regiments of
infantry and over 3,000 horse across the River Tweed. The
men were described as raw, untrained and undisciplined and
were led by inefficient officers, but they did constitute
additional manpower and their appearance on the scene
meant that the Marquess of Newcastle was now fighting a
war on two fronts.

Leven's progress, through snow and floods, was slow but,
on 3 February, he reached the town of Newcastle. The
Marquess of Newcastle had arrived the day before and, as
Leven's siege guns did not get there until 7 February, he had
time to piece together a defence. The northern suburbs were
burnt so as to deprive the besiegers of cover, and ships at

anchor in the River Tyne were scuttled to pre-empt a seaborne assault. Thinking that the prevalent atrocious weather would prevent the Scots moving further south, Newcastle relaxed his surveillance of their positions. However, Leven had no intention of being tied down by protracted siege operations and took advantage of his opponent's error of judgement. Leaving a small force to continue the siege, he led his main army across the icy River Tyne and on into Durham.

In Cheshire also, the fighting season was starting early – and with similar unfortunate results for the Royalists. Sir John Byron, who had been created 'Field Marshal of Wales and the Marches', was determined to make the most of the infusion of English troops returning from service in Ireland. The first batch, comprising 3,000 infantry and a few horse had recently arrived, but to ensure the unhindered movement of such valuable reinforcements, it was necessary to take Nantwich, currently in Roundhead hands. Byron attacked the town on 17 January, but was repulsed with heavy losses. To add to his woes, on 24 January, Sir Thomas Fairfax arrived hotfoot from Lincolnshire to join forces with Sir William Brereton. Fairfax's men were poorly provisioned and armed – he had used his own money to buy new uniforms for them – but Byron was well outnumbered.

The siege was lifted and Byron rode out to meet Fairfax to the north-west of the town, near Acton village. The conditions for fighting were anything but ideal. Snow lay upon the ground, the River Weaver was overflowing and the ground was intersected by hedged enclosures, but Byron went onto the offensive. Pushing forward on the Royalist left, he was challenged and driven back by Sir William Fairfax's cavalry. The battle on the Royalist right was a more confused affair, but the Parliamentarian infantry stood firm, repelling an assault by the Irish contingent. The outcome was decided by the appearance of 800 musketeers from the Nantwich garrison, who took the Royalist infantry on the right flank, breaking all resistance. Byron managed to withdraw with much of his own regiment intact, but over 1,500 Royalists were captured, including a number who had taken refuge in Acton church. To add insult to injury, half of the prisoners changed colours and joined Fairfax.

On the political front, the King attempted to make progress by calling an Oxford Parliament. In the absence of Pym, it was hoped, the Commons could be brought to heel. Undoubtedly, it was a good idea and was intended to focus opposition to what the Royalists saw as the Scottish invasion of England. Comprising many of the MPs who had deserted what Charles called the 'pretended Parliament' at Westminster, it met on 22 January. A letter was sent to the Earl of Essex inviting him to attend peace talks, but the Westminster MPs refused to acknowledge the legality of the Oxford assembly. On 16 April, it was adjourned, having achieved nothing.

On the day the Oxford Parliament convened, Oliver Cromwell received his commission as Lieutenant-General of the Army of the Eastern Association. Its commander, the Earl of Manchester, had already created an effective fighting force from the patchwork of East Anglian county recruits, but it was Cromwell who would later receive much of the credit. Cromwell was also made a member of the 'Committee of Both Kingdoms'. Authorised on 16 February, this was essentially a war cabinet consisting of nominees from both Houses of Parliament, together with Scottish representatives, brought together for the purpose of 'better managing the affairs of both nations in the common cause, according to the ends expressed in the late covenant and treaty between the two nations of England and Scotland'.

On 1 February, Charles made a significant military appointment of his own. James Graham, the Earl of Montrose, received a commission as Lieutenant-General of Royalist forces in Scotland, a somewhat empty title as the King's forces in Scotland were non-existent. However, the energy and commitment of Montrose were destined to bring hope to Charles when all seemed lost south of the border.

The onset of spring and the start of the campaigning season brought no relief to the King's woes. On 29 March, Waller and Hopton met again – this time at Cheriton in Sussex. Waller was still smarting from his defeat at Roundway Down and, despite a numerical advantage, preferred to avoid a pitched battle but Hopton, reinforced by the Earl of Forth, was determined to force the issue. Both armies occupied high ground, Hopton to the north of Cheriton, and Waller with the village on his left flank and Cheriton Wood on his right. A depression in the ground divided them. Waller took control of the wood, but his men were driven out and, from a position of some strength, Hopton decided to stand firm to await an attack. Unfortunately, one of his officers, Colonel Henry Bard, decided to take the initiative by assaulting Waller's right wing. His charge was met by Sir Arthur Haselrig's cuirassiers, upon whom Bard's men were unable to make any impression. Royalist cavalry attempting to ride to Bard's aid along a narrow lane (their only means of descent) were thrown into disarray by the enemy horse. With the Roundhead infantry now advancing along the entire front, Hopton decided to withdraw to Alresford.

Cheriton was in no way a decisive encounter. Casualties on both sides were comparatively light and Waller did not follow up his advantage, but Hopton's army had been thrown back onto the defensive and the threat of a Royalist advance on London was neutralised for the time being.

*

In the North, matters were coming to a head. The Marquess of Newcastle was preoccupied with the Scots and it was left to Sir John Belasyse to consolidate the Royalist position in Yorkshire. Such Royalist garrisons as remained in the East and West Ridings were scattered and under-strength, and the Parliamentarians had little difficulty in picking them off, one by one. Ultimately, Belasyse set up his field command at Selby to await developments.

Sir Thomas Fairfax – Belasyse's cousin – was under orders to proceed north to assist the Scots whose progress south was painfully slow but, at Ferrybridge, he fell in with his father and together they decided to attack Selby. On 11 April, they assaulted three of the four entrances to the town. For upwards of two hours, the Royalists stood firm until Lord Fairfax's own division managed to force one of the defensive barricades blocking the narrow streets. This enabled Sir Thomas to lead his cavalry between the houses and the river bank. A counter-charge led by Belasyse himself resulted in a tense moment when Sir Thomas was unhorsed, but his men fought their way forward and, pressing on, drove the Royalists across the River Ouse and on towards York. A Parliamentarian siege of York was now inevitable.

With a garrison only five hundred strong, the city was vulnerable. When Newcastle received the news, he moved south, outmarching the Scots, and entered the city with some 4,000 infantry on 16 April. He sent a message to the King, advising him that he expected to be able to hold out for a maximum of six weeks. Between 21 and 23 April, the Fairfaxes effectively sealed off York to the east. The Earl of Leven, who had followed in Newcastle's wake, besieged the city from the west and the south. The gap to the north was plugged by the Earl of Manchester's army, which arrived on 4 June.

The city itself was built to withstand a siege and, even though he was surrounded by three armies, Newcastle could afford to play a waiting game. He gained a valuable week by engaging in fruitless negotiations, and the single assault made on the city, when it did come, was beaten off. Although the 'spotted fever' was in evidence among the garrison, it was also rife in the ranks of the besiegers, particularly among the Scots. In addition, the Fairfaxes complained that they were running short of ammunition and that their men were owed four months' back pay. (The cost of keeping their army in the field amounted to £15,000 per month.) Then came reports that 17,500 Royalists under the command of Prince Rupert were approaching Knaresborough...

*

Rupert held a roving brief. He could turn up anywhere at any time, and frequently did so. On 6 February, he set out to try to salvage the declining situation in the north-west and, by 19 February, he was establishing his headquarters in Shrewsbury. A month later, he was on his way to Newark, where the Royalist garrison was under siege. His arrival on nearby Beacon Hill on the morning of 21 March caught the Parliamentarian commander conducting the siege, Sir John Meldrum, completely unawares. Consolidating his position in the Northgate area of the town, Meldrum sent a body of horse to halt Rupert's progress. The Prince met it head on, driving it back into the town. On cue, the Royalist garrison sallied forth and Meldrum, fearful of annihilation amid the twin-pronged assault, surrendered. His army – less 200 casualties, 3,000 muskets, 11 cannon and 2 mortars – was permitted to retire. It was a famous victory: the Parliamentarian garrison in Lincoln, in fear of imminent attack, abandoned ship, while the garrisons at Nottingham and Derby made ready to repel boarders.

After the success at Newark, it was back to Shrewsbury and then, on 25 April, Rupert visited Oxford to attend a council of war. The Royalist capital was looking increasingly fragile and Rupert advised strengthening the garrison, along with those of Wallingford, Abingdon, Reading and Banbury, and, in addition, keeping a mobile body of cavalry in the area. His advice was taken and he returned to Shrewsbury on 5 May. As soon as he had gone, the plan was changed and Reading and Abingdon were abandoned. It was all very well to talk about strengthening garrisons, but where was the manpower to be found?

On 3 June, rather than risk being boxed in at Oxford, the King marched out with some 3,000 infantry and 4,000 horse. After weeks of ineffective manoeuvring, he met Sir William Waller's army at Cropredy Bridge, near Banbury. In the early hours of 29 June, Waller occupied a commanding position on Crouch Hill, to the south-west of Banbury. In an effort to draw him away from this advantageous ground, Charles marched away in the direction of Daventry. Waller gingerly took the bait, electing to shadow the Royalists by marching almost parallel with them along the Southam road and separated from them only by the River Cherwell. As the roads approached one another, Waller noted that the

Royalists were well strung-out and he decided to try to cut off Lord Wilmot's rearguard from the rest of the column. Charles had already crossed the Cherwell at Hay's Bridge, to the north, and when Waller reached Cropredy Bridge to the south, he sent Lieutenant-General John Middleton across to make a dash for Hay's Bridge, take it and hold it. Waller himself crossed the river further south, at Slat Mill, to take Wilmot in the rear.

There was nothing wrong with the strategy, but the Royalists were not caught unawares. As Waller crossed the ford at Slat Mill, he was attacked by the (new) Earl of Northampton. At the same time, the Earl of Cleveland attacked Middleton as he sped towards Hay's Bridge. In addition, the Royalist vanguard had re-crossed the river and was also bearing down on Middleton, who was forced back over Cropredy Bridge. Waller, too, was pushed back over the Cherwell. Their tasks successfully completed, Cleveland and Northampton pulled back to regroup.

The Royalists made much of Cropredy Bridge, for their success guaranteed the immediate security of Oxford, and the victory has occasionally been cited by military historians as an example of the King's competent generalship, although the encounter itself was a minor one, with Roundhead casualties numbering around 200 dead and wounded. Within a few days, moreover, such comfort as the Royalists chose to draw from their modest achievement would be eclipsed by the despair attendant upon catastrophic events involving Rupert at York.

*

After leaving Oxford, Rupert had returned to Shrewsbury to prepare for an expedition to bolster the Royalist war effort in Lancashire. He set out on 16 May, at the head of

6,000 foot and 2,000 horse. By 22 May, he had reached Sandbach and was at Knutsford the day after. At Stockport, he trounced a 3,000-strong Parliamentarian force and was able to relieve Lathom House, ably defended by the Countess of Derby and under siege since February. When the Royalists arrived at Lathom on 25 May, the besiegers, led by Colonel Alexander Rigby, retreated to Bolton which Rupert, accompanied by the Earl of Derby, proceeded to storm. In what has been described as the worst authorised massacre of the war, several hundred defenders were slaughtered. (The Earl of Derby, furious at finding a former servant fighting for the opposition, ran the man through with his sword.) Although the magnitude of the offence was probably exaggerated, it did nothing to win any new support for the Royalist cause in staunchly Parliamentarian Bolton.

From Bolton, Rupert marched on to Bury, where he was met by Goring's cavalry. At Wigan, he received an enthusiastic welcome – less so at Parliamentarian Liverpool. It was while he was at Liverpool that he received from his uncle a letter purporting to give him instructions on how to proceed: 'If York be lost,' said Charles, 'I shall esteem my crown little less, unless supported by your sudden march to me, and a miraculous conquest in the South, before the effects of the Northern power can be found here; but if York be relieved, and you beat the rebel Armies of Both Kingdoms, which are before it, then but otherwise not, I may possibly make a shift to spin out time until you come to assist me: Wherefore I command and conjure you immediately march with all your force to the relief of York; but if that be either lost, or have freed themselves from the besiegers, or that for want of powder you cannot undertake that work, that you immediately march, with your whole strength to Worcester, to assist me and my army...'

What was Rupert to do? It was open to him to change course and march south, but the King was obviously hoping that he could work a miracle at York. The notion had been presented as a challenge, and he accepted it. It would have been foolish to expect that a man of his temperament could do otherwise, and so he continued on his way. His march towards the city was a tour de force in itself. From Liverpool, he marched to Preston, then on to Clitheroe and Gisburn in Yorkshire. On 26 June, he arrived at Skipton Castle, where he remained for three days while his growing army was drilled and messengers were sent on to York. Moving on, he reached Denton – one of the Fairfax estates – on 29 June. The next day, he was at Knaresborough Castle, ready to advance on York, just fourteen miles away.

Not unnaturally, the besiegers were convinced that Rupert intended to launch an attack from the direction of Knaresborough. In order to block his path, they marched out to Marston Moor, an expanse of heath seven miles to the west of the city. Unexpectedly, the Prince swung north to cross the River Ure at Boroughbridge and the River Swale at Thornton Bridge. On 1 July, Goring was sent ahead to order Newcastle to be ready to march against the allies at 4 o'clock the following morning.

The allies themselves passed an uneasy night on the moor, pondering Rupert's next move. They decided to cut him off from the south by blocking the road at Selby. Accordingly, in the morning, the main body of the army marched out, leaving 4,000 dragoons behind. It was expected that enemy scouting parties would be seen but, with the allied column strung out vulnerably along its line of march, more and more Royalists began to appear on the northern fringes of the moor. It soon became apparent that Rupert's whole army was on the way. Luckily for the allies, Rupert could do nothing until Newcastle's troops appeared, and they straggled in slowly throughout the course of the day.

Regrouping, the allies, 27,000 strong, drew up to the south of the Long Marston to Tockwith road, while the Royalist army of 20,000 men deployed on the north side. For Parliament, Cromwell and Sir David Leslie occupied the left wing, with Sir Thomas Fairfax and Major-General John Lambert on the right. In the middle, and to the fore, was the massed infantry of Lieutenant-General William Baillie and Sergeant-Major General Lawrence Crawford. To the rear were the infantry of Lord Fairfax and the Earl of Manchester. For the Royalists, the cavalry of Lord Byron (Sir John had been given a peerage in October 1643) and Lord Molyneux were on the right, with Goring and Sir Charles Lucas on the left, while the infantry of Major-General Henry Tillier, Sir William Blakeston, Sir Francis Mackworth and Colonel Thomas Napier occupied the centre ground.

Preliminary manoeuvres having taken up the best part of the day – it was now approaching 7 o'clock on the evening of 2 July – Newcastle asked Rupert whether he intended to give battle that night. Rupert replied that the following morning would be soon enough, and Newcastle retired to his coach to smoke a pipe. Each man made himself as comfortable as circumstances permitted. Newcastle, admittedly more comfortable than anyone else, had barely lit his pipe when he heard 'a great noise and thunder of shooting'. Rupert had got it wrong.

On the other side of the road, there had been no laxness. With Royalists still arriving on the field, Leven grasped the opportunity to catch the enemy off guard, and the allies unsportingly began moving forward. It was Cromwell who made the first contact on the allied left wing. Byron, who was in a state of readiness, advanced to meet him, but his cavalry became bogged down in marshy ground. In an attempt to bolster Byron's crumbling line, Rupert left his command post, arriving on the scene with his own Life Guard. Cromwell, probably supported by Sir David Leslie, eventually broke through, sending the Royalist right wing, including Rupert, reeling back towards Wilstrop Wood in the rear.

On the allied right, however, Sir Thomas Fairfax came to grief. His cavalry experienced difficulties negotiating a ditch, thus allowing Goring to get his act together, and they suffered heavy casualties. Goring then charged through the allied lines, some of his men continuing on to attack their baggage train. In the centre, the allied infantry were pushed back, many of them deserting the field. Their generals panicked, Leven fleeing towards Leeds, while Lord Fairfax made for his home near Cawood where, according to his enemies, he went straight to bed.

Meanwhile, Cromwell had been absent from the battle. Having sustained a minor neck wound, he had retired to a cottage in Tockwith to have it dressed, but he was soon back in the saddle. Now, he led his regiment around to the rear of the Royalist lines to challenge Goring who, considering the battle won, was taken off guard. Thus encouraged, the allied infantry regrouped and pressed forward. Within a very short time, what had appeared to be a victory for the Royalists developed into a defeat. At length, the only Royalists standing their ground were Newcastle's own 'Whitecoat' regiment. To preserve their honour, as well as to cover the Royalist retreat, they refused all offers of quarter and died almost to the last man. When all was over, Royalist dead totalled 4,000, while the allies lost as few as 300. It is said that Rupert evaded capture by hiding in a beanfield.

Analysts have long wrangled over the question of Rupert's failure. His reputation as an invincible opponent lay in tatters, but he was ill suited to take command of a major set-piece confrontation. In smaller encounters such as Chalgrove Field, his customary dashing cavalry charge would invariably win the day whereas at Marston Moor his preoccupation with one portion of the action had disastrous consequences. He wasted no time in rallying the remains of his army – some 6,000 men – and marching westward, abandoning York to its fate, but living to fight another day. Neither did the allies waste any time in resuming the siege. The governor, Sir Thomas Glemham, was called upon to surrender, but he refused. Instead, he hurriedly penned a letter to the King, begging for more help. When it became evident that nothing else could be done, an honourable surrender was arranged in order to save the city from destruction and its citizens from further hardship. Newcastle also threw in the towel. Worn out by the professional and personal responsibilities of command, and with only £90 in his pocket, he took a ship from Scarborough, to begin life in exile on the Continent.

He was not alone, for on 14 July, two days before the surrender of York, Queen Henrietta Maria embarked for France. She had left Oxford in April to travel to Exeter where, on 16 June, in the comparative safety of the Royalist south-west, she gave birth to a daughter, Henrietta. The delivery had not been an easy one, and she appealed to the

Earl of Essex to grant her safe conduct to Bath so that she might take the waters. Essex refused, but he did propose taking her to London where, he said, she might seek medical advice – an offer which she herself wisely declined. Instead, she made her way to Falmouth, where she sailed for Brest, leaving behind her new-born child. Although she did not know it at the time, she would never see her husband again.

*

The first half of 1644 had proved disastrous for the Royalists, but the latter portion of the year offered more promise. The army of Prince Maurice, 6,000 strong, was occupied in a siege of Lyme in Dorset, and Parliament resolved to relieve the town. It was intended that Sir William Waller would command the expedition, but Essex took on the job personally – a decision he would have cause to regret. He began his march on 6 June, but so fluid was the situation that, within a few weeks, Prince Maurice had raised the siege at Lyme, while the defeat of Waller's army at Cropredy Bridge enabled the King to change tack and follow Essex to the south-west.

Essex might have turned his attention to Exeter, but decided to embark on the far more ambitious project of securing Cornwall. On 2 August, he received news that the armies of the King and Prince Maurice had linked up and were on his trail. Having arranged to meet ships of the Earl of Warwick's Parliamentarian fleet at Fowey, however, he was not unduly worried. He did not know that unfavourable westerlies were keeping Warwick at anchor in Portsmouth. The cavalry had been on the way – specifically Lieutenant-General John Middleton with 2,000 men – but they had been halted at Bridgwater. Essex was on his own.

He advanced to Lostwithiel, which he took and planned to

defend, setting up strong-points at nearby Restmorel Castle and on Beacon Hill. Advancing slowly but surely, however, Charles consolidated his position and, on 6 August, with Essex boxed in, he felt sufficiently confident to offer terms of surrender. Essex refused them but he made no attempt to engage the Royalists, who were permitted to establish themselves along the banks of the Fowey.

On 21 August, Sir Richard Grenville drove the Parliamentarians from Beacon Hill and from Restmorel Castle. On 26 August, Goring took St Blazey on the west of the Fowey. For some time, the Royalist lines had been over-stretched, but Essex still balked at the idea of breaking out. In the end, he compromised. Sir William Balfour led his cavalry to safety during the night of 31 August, while Essex, still entertaining vague hopes that Warwick would appear, retreated to Fowey. Without cavalry cover, the infantry stood little chance of survival. Constantly harassed by the Royalist horse, they had to ditch artillery and supplies. A rearguard action at Castle Dore held the Royalists temporarily, but the end was near.

At dawn, in the company of two of his senior subordinates, Lord Robartes and Sir John Meyrick, Essex deserted his command, slipping away to Plymouth on a fishing boat. Philip Skippon was left to negotiate the best terms he could on behalf of his infantry. An agreement was reached whereby his men were permitted to lay down their arms and march away, on the understanding that they would not fight against the King until they had reached Southampton or Portsmouth. This decision has often been criticised as being unduly lenient, but Charles lacked the resources to cater for 6,000 prisoners and, although they were the enemy, he still considered them his own subjects.

As it was, despite having been promised safe conduct, the refugees suffered dreadfully. Attacked by Royalist troops and sympathisers, starving and without shelter, up to a third of them perished before reaching their destination. Essex returned to London. Many another man would – and should – have been court-martialled, but he laid the blame for the disaster upon his subordinates. Parliament was just thankful that he had not fallen into enemy hands.

The capture of 6,000 men, 10,000 weapons, 36 cannon and cartloads of supplies at Fowey demonstrated that the Royalists were not yet beaten. Then, hard on the heels of the victory at Lostwithiel came another, more than 500 miles away – at Tippermuir, near Perth. Initially, the Earl of Montrose had been able to make little impression upon the might of the Covenanters in Scotland. Then, the Royalist Earl of Antrim, who had faced similar difficulties in Ireland, persuaded the fearless warrior, Alasdair MacDonald, to lead a motley force of 1,000 men across the Irish Sea. MacDonald's family had been ousted from their homeland by the Campbells and Alasdair viewed the adventure largely as an opportunity to gain revenge. Together, MacDonald and Montrose would prove a force to be reckoned with.

Their first test was formidable enough. At Perth lay the Covenanter army of Lord Elcho – 7,000 foot and upwards of 700 horse, with nine pieces of artillery. Between them, Montrose and MacDonald could muster no more than 3,000 foot, armed with muskets (for which each man had only a single round), swords, bows and arrows and clubs. Nevertheless, Montrose chose to challenge the vastly superior force. On 1 September, on the wide plain of Tippermuir, Montrose spread his men thinly – three deep – to avoid being outflanked. Elcho sent forward skimishers, which Montrose drove back. As they retired in confusion, the skirmishers disordered their own front line. Then the whole Royalist army launched a charge, waiting until the last possible moment before firing their single volley and then following through with clubbed musket and dirk. Elcho's cavalry attempted to regroup, but when Montrose seized the high ground, the Covenanters scattered. Guns, ammunition and supplies were the reward of the victors. Some 2,000 Covenanters are said to have been killed, along with many townsfolk who, following the custom of the time, had come to watch the battle. The victory did not result in a clamorous rush to the Royal Standard, but it did demonstrate that the King's cause in Scotland, as in England, although still on the critical list, was far from dead and buried.

Indeed, the relations between the Scots and Parliament were never cordial. Although the Committee of Both Kingdoms was still intact, tensions did occur, as they did on 13 September with the passage through Parliament of the 'Toleration Order' (also known as the 'Accommodation Order') which was concerned with the ordination of ministers of religion. During the debate, fears were voiced that one kind of tyranny might replace another, in the form of ministers who might choose to wield the power enjoyed by bishops. Cromwell, who was present, suggested that the Committee of Both Kingdoms might wish to take into consideration 'differences of opinion' in Church government and, if a union were not possible, to find a way in which 'tender consciences who cannot in all things submit to the common rule which shall be established, may be borne with'. The principle was accepted – something that was not lost on the Scots who decried the idea of having 'liberty for all religions without any exceptions'. For the moment, however, it was still necessary to maintain a united front against Catholicism and High Church Anglicanism, and matters did not come to a head.

The final battle of the calendar year occurred at Newbury. Charles intended to relieve the Royalist garrisons of Banbury Castle, Basing House and Donnington Castle, all of which were under threat. Fearing that the King intended to make another attempt on London, Parliament joined together the armies of Manchester, Waller and Essex. In all, some 20,000 men met at Basingstoke on 20 October. Charles had been able to do nothing for Basing House, but he detached a portion of his army to relieve the pressure on Banbury while he proceeded to Donnington Castle. His approach was sufficient to free up Donnington's garrison and, on 22 October, he retired to Newbury, his army between the town and Donnington to the north. It was a well chosen position, the army's flanks being protected by the Rivers Lambourne and Kennet.

When the Parliamentarians arrived, they resolved to divide their force. Waller would march around the Royalist army, to face them from the west, while Manchester would deploy his troops to the east. It was known that the Royalists would be prepared, but with a 2:1 numerical advantage, the Parliamentarians had to attack. Manchester's assault on the morning of 27 October made little impression on Sir George Lisle's strong defences. Waller was being harassed by Prince Maurice even before he was in position, and he was not ready to do anything before the afternoon. Although Maurice was well placed on Speen Hill, Phillip Skippon's infantry made a determined assault which threw him back.

Had Manchester renewed his attack to the east, the

Royalists would have been hard pressed, yet he failed to do so. Then Waller's cavalry, led by Cromwell and Sir William Balfour, came to grief as they tried, unsuccessfully, to negotiate a mix of enclosures and marshland. As the daylight was fading, Manchester did attack, but it was too late. In the growing darkness, the fighting on both fronts died down and, despite being hemmed in, the Royalists managed to slip away during the night, taking the road to Oxford and safety. This time, Manchester took the blame for the Parliamentarian failure, Essex having had the good sense to miss the affair by falling ill.

With the ragged remnants of both armies of 1644 retiring into winter quarters, the negotiating table replaced the battlefield as the arena of operations. The Scots were keen to further the aims of the Solemn League and Covenant and were instrumental in initiating more peace proposals, known as 'The Propositions of Uxbridge'. The King was asked to 'swear and sign the late Solemn League and Covenant' and an Act was to be passed 'to make void the Irish Cessation and all treaties with the rebels without consent of both Houses of Parliament'. In the event of an agreement being reached, there was an extensive list of those 'who shall expect no pardon'. Included were the Princes Rupert and Maurice, the Marquess of Newcastle, William Laud and several leading field commanders – among them Montrose, Goring, Hopton, Widdrington, Langdale, Byron and the Hothams. There was also a demand for the perpetual suppression of stage plays.

In response, Charles demanded that his 'own revenue, magazines, towns, forts and ships' be restored to him immediately, together with his 'known power and rights', and promised to consent to 'any good Acts to be made for the suppression of Popery, and for the firmer settling of the Protestant religion established by law'. Echoing Cromwell, he also suggested the framing of legislation 'for the ease of tender consciences, in such particulars as shall be agreed upon'. In so doing, he may have hoped to exploit the divisions between the allies on the contentious issue of toleration. While there was still a chance of victory by force of arms, however, neither side was interested in compromise, and the half-hearted discussions were abandoned in February 1645.

1645: Check

The beginning of March 1645, your father went to Bristol... I then lying-in of my first son, Harrison Fanshawe, who was born on 22 February, he left me behind him: as for that, it was the first time we had parted a day since we married. He was extremely afflicted, even to tears, though passion was against his nature; but the sense of leaving me with a dying child, which did die two days after, in a garrison town, extremely weak and very poor, were such circumstances as he could not bear with, only the argument of necessity

Memoirs of Ann, Lady Fanshawe

January opened with a few executions to help concentrate the minds of those who might be considering forsaking Parliament. On 2 January, Sir John Hotham, ex-Governor of Hull, was executed on Tower Hill for planning to 'turn' Hull. His son had been executed the day before. On 10 January, after four years' detention in the Tower, Laud was executed. During his trial for High Treason, his accusers were unable to prove him guilty and, as in the case of Strafford, they had to resort to a Bill of Attainder. On this occasion, however, the King was not on hand to give his consent.

Militarily, the Earl of Leven had succeeded in lending enough weight to the Parliamentarian effort to bring victory in the North. It was hoped to persuade the Scots to move further south but the threat posed by Montrose made Leven reluctant to do so. In fact, he found it necessary to weaken his army by ordering forces under Baillie and Hurry – now fighting for the Covenanters – to return to Scotland to deal with him.

On 2 February, Montrose was in action again, at Inverlochy Castle, near Fort William. The Covenanter Marquess of Argyll had withdrawn to his quarters on board a vessel in Loch Linnhe. Although his absence was attributed to cowardice, he had been injured in a fall from his horse. Sir Duncan Campbell of Auchinbreck assumed temporary command, forming his troops – nearly 4,000 of them – into solid ranks. Montrose, with only 1,500 men, was thought to stand little chance. However, Magnus O'Cahan led a furious charge which broke Auchinbreck's right wing, while the dependable Alasdair MacDonald achieved a similar feat on the left. Montrose led his main body of infantry in an attack on Auchinbreck's centre, pushing the front lines back onto those in the rear. Even so, the Covenanters – in particular the Campbells – rallied to put up a fight, as Montrose observed, 'like men with a better cause'. Argyll sailed away down the loch, abandoning his men. 1,500 of them were cut down and Montrose celebrated another victory.

In England, the Parliamentarians were busy reorganising their own forces. They had learned the lessons of the previous year, fully realising that an efficient, professional army was required if their objectives were to be met. The result was the constitution, on 15 February 1645, of the New Model Army. The core comprised veterans of the armies commanded by Essex, Manchester and Waller, their numbers augmented by conscription to a projected total of 22,000. There would be regular pay (at a cost of £56,000 per month) and a well-structured chain of command with promotion strictly on merit. The man chosen to lead this revolutionary force was Sir Thomas Fairfax. He had proved himself to be an able soldier and, just as important as far as his political masters were concerned, he harboured no political ambitions of his own.

Coupled with the formation of the New Model Army was an interesting piece of legislation known as the Self-Denying Ordinance by which members of both the House of Commons and the House of Lords were to be 'discharged... of and from all and every office or command military or civil'. This meant that the likes of Essex, Manchester, Waller and Cromwell would have to choose between their positions as MPs and their military commands. All opted for their parliamentary seats.

The absence of so many experienced hands and, at the other end of the scale, the inclusion of so many inexperienced recruits, endowed the fledgling New Model Army with an initial vulnerability which the Royalists were quick to exploit. On 29 May, a Royalist army, led by the King and Prince Rupert, appeared outside Parliamentarian Leicester. The following morning, Rupert offered the town a free pardon with leave for the Parliamentarian cavalry to depart – if they would surrender. The terms were refused and the Royalists attacked. The garrison put up a stout defence, women bringing up bales of wool to stuff the holes made in the walls by the besieging artillery. Fierce fighting continued after the walls were successfully stormed, the last stand taking place in St Martin's church. Charles spent two nights at the abbey as a guest of the Duchess of Devonshire, but he had no sooner departed than his men crowned an orgy of pillage by burning his hostess's mansion.

In London, there was consternation. The City demanded

that the New Model Army be free to act 'without attending commands and directions from remote councils' (ie the advisory Committee of Both Kingdoms). Yielding to public opinion, the Committee informed Fairfax that they had decided to remove 'all limitations or restrictions under which you may be placed by former letters, leaving it wholly to you who are upon the spot to do what by the advice of your council of war you shall judge most conducive to the public interest.' Fairfax thought it in the public interest to have Cromwell as his Lieutenant-General of Horse and, despite the restrictions imposed by the Self-Denying Ordinance, proposed him for the post. The Committee had little option but to approve the appointment.

The Royalist victory at Leicester had been preceded just a few days earlier by another triumph for Montrose in Scotland. On the evening of 8 May, his army bivouacked at the village of Auldearn, two miles to the east of Nairn. Hurry, fielding 3,500 infantry and 400 horse, made a night march in heavy rain from Inverness. He should have been able to take Montrose by surprise, but his musketeers tested their damp weapons by firing them, thus alerting the Royalist camp. Accustomed to reacting quickly, Montrose was able to deploy his men before Hurry's arrival. Despite having only 2,000 infantry and 250 horse, Montrose made the astonishing decision to divide his command. MacDonald, with 500 men, took up a position to the north of the village while Montrose, with the main body, concealed himself to the east. Advancing from the south-west, the Covenanters deployed on the high ground of Garlic Hill, funnelling their men into a narrow front to face MacDonald's entrenched position.

As Hurry's infantry advanced, MacDonald charged out to

meet them, but was driven back by sheer weight of numbers. At this point, Montrose unleashed his cavalry which bore down on Hurry's cavalry protecting the Covenanters' right wing. The unexpected assault caused them to sheer away, leaving their infantry open to attack. On a field of battle so confined as that of Auldearn, it was natural that confusion should result when the Covenanters' right wing was turned in upon the centre, thus precluding Hurry from the effective deployment of his reserves. The commitment of the Royalist infantry under the leadership of MacDonald, who rallied his men for a renewed attack, eventually wore down the resolve of the Covenanters in the rear, many of whom would have been unable to strike a blow while the fighting was at its height. In the end, they sought to save themselves, leaving Montrose in possession of the field. Hurry, belying his name, was one of the last to flee.

The Battle of Auldearn is universally regarded as Montrose's greatest battle and has been described as the most brilliant victory of the Civil War. However, there was a downside in that many of Montrose's Highlanders tended to view the spoils of battle – in this case the capture of Hurry's baggage train – as the sole objective of the campaign and, once enriched, they made their way home, thus exacerbating their leader's ongoing manpower crisis.

While Charles may have taken comfort from Leicester and Auldearn, neither occasion advanced his cause to any great extent. With the benefit of hindsight, it can be argued that, for Parliament, the loss of Leicester was an inconvenience and the defeat at Auldearn an irrelevance. Summer was approaching and no major battle between the leading protagonists had yet been fought, but this was soon to be remedied with the meeting of the King's army and the

as-yet-untried New Model Army at the Northamptonshire
village of Naseby.

*

The strategy behind the Royalist assault on Leicester lay in
the need to relieve some of the growing pressure on Oxford.
It worked – but not necessarily to the King's advantage.
While he tarried in Daventry, Fairfax was exploiting the free
hand he had been given by the Committee of Both
Kingdoms, by marching to meet him. On the morning of 13
June, Charles moved out of Daventry in the direction of
Market Harborough, ignorant of the fact that Fairfax was
now only ten miles away at Kislingbury. Rupert spent the
night of 13 June in Market Harborough, while Charles
himself slept at Lubbenham, two miles to the west. A section
of the Royalist rearguard was in Naseby, where they were
captured while playing darts at a local inn by an advance
Parliamentarian party commanded by Colonel Henry Ireton.
When this intelligence reached Charles, he had to decide
whether to return to Leicester, in the hope of picking up
reinforcements, or to give battle. Rupert was of the opinion
that it would be wiser to avoid a confrontation at this
juncture, but others convinced the King that he should stand
and fight. And so, in the early hours of 14 June, the Royalists
prepared to move south, to meet Fairfax in the vicinity of
Naseby.

Charles enjoyed the advantage of being able to choose his
ground, and Rupert identified Dust Hill, a ridge one and a
half miles to the north of Naseby, as an appropriate site. The
Royalists duly deployed along the ridge – Sir Marmaduke
Langdale's horse on the left and Prince Rupert on the right,
with Astley's infantry in the middle. Fairfax drew up
opposite, on Red Hill – Cromwell commanding the right

wing and Ireton on the left, with Skippon's infantry facing Astley. In addition, a line of dragoons under Colonel John Okey was concealed behind a hedge on the extreme left, with some 300 musketeers deployed well to the fore of the infantry line. Both sides held reserves in the rear – the King was positioned with the Royalist reserve. The King was outnumbered with, perhaps, 10,000 men as opposed to Fairfax's 14,000. Whatever the Royalists lacked in numbers was more than compensated for in experience and enthusiasm, personified in Rupert's irresistible panache and the indefatigable resolution of Astley. The New Model Army comprised many raw recruits and, by his deployment of dragoons and musketeers, Fairfax must have hoped to take the edge off the fearsome prospect of one of Rupert's devastating cavalry charges and a relentless infantry advance by Astley.

Shortly before 10 o'clock on the morning of 14 June, Fairfax withdrew Skippon's infantry from view and it is sometimes argued that Rupert, duped into thinking that a full retreat was under way, embarked upon a premature advance. Whatever his reasons, advance he did. Okey claimed that the concentrated fire of his dragoons took much of the sting out of Rupert's onslaught, but Ireton's cavalry was still swept away. Instead of turning in on Skippon's infantry, Rupert sped on, through the Parliamentarian lines, as far as Naseby, where an attempt was made to take the enemy's baggage train. Back on the battlefield, Astley's infantry, striding out purposefully, locked horns with Skippon. Wounded by a musket ball, Skippon refused to leave the field, but his men were nevertheless deprived of effective leadership. Astley tried to press home the advantage, but an attack on his right flank by Ireton with the remains of his cavalry held him in check. On the Parliamentarian right, Cromwell charged — and overwhelmed — Langdale, who was at the disadvantage of having to advance uphill.

The outcome was determined by the use made of the reserves. Fairfax used his reserves expediently, introducing three regiments of foot which helped to push back the Royalist infantry. Similarly, to ensure against the possibility of Langdale regrouping, two regiments of horse were sent to outflank him. The Royalist reserves, meanwhile, remained immobile on Dust Hill. Ultimately, Rupert succeeded in rallying his men and regained the battlefield, only to discover that the outcome had already been determined. In a repeat of Edgehill, there was little that Rupert's exhausted cavalry could do. Instead of riding to the hard-pressed Astley's aid, therefore, he returned to the King's side where, together, they watched the systematic destruction of their gallant infantry, now beset on all sides.

Inclined towards making a last-ditch attempt to save the day, Charles placed himself at the head of his own Life Guard, as if in the act of spearheading one final charge. He was stopped by the Earl of Carnwath who took hold of his bridle, saying 'Will you go upon your death in an instant?' In so doing, he turned the King's horse. The Royalist reserves, growing increasingly agitated as the situation deteriorated, turned and ran, having interpreted the manoeuvre as a signal to retire. The retreat became general, the Parliamentarians harrying the fleeing Royalists — along a line of withdrawal punctuated by solid rearguard actions — as far as Great Glen, two miles short of Leicester.

The short-term results of Naseby were severe enough for the Royalists — a seasoned army routed, 1,000 dead, 5,000 taken prisoner and 100 camp followers butchered for good measure. In the long term, the King's private papers, which had been with his baggage train, did much harm. Consisting, in part, of letters to the Queen, the incriminating documents dealt with plans to call in French mercenaries and, worse still, the solicitation of discontented Irish Catholics, with the promise of a repeal of the recusancy laws. With the battered remnants of his army in tow, Charles now repaired to South Wales, from where, with the aid of Goring's army – engaged in a fruitless siege of Taunton – he might have mounted one final offensive. Instead, he wavered, idling away four crucial weeks at Raglan Castle, before embarking on a series of perambulations, allegedly with the continuing aim of regrouping but, realistically, in the vain hope of evading inevitable capture.

On the other hand, Naseby proved to be the making of the New Model Army. Experienced cavalry had contributed greatly to the victory, but the infantry gained precious experience and the confidence which results from the defeat of formidable opponents. Cromwell later remarked, 'When I saw the enemy draw up and march in gallant order towards us, and we a company of poor ignorant men... I could not... but smile out to God in praises, in assurance of victory.' Perhaps his trust in God had been strengthened in the knowledge that the Royalists were so obviously outnumbered.

*

The cat and mouse game in which the King and Parliament were now involved had been played by Montrose since the commencement of his campaign. In the weeks following Naseby, Montrose and Baillie had been stalking each other through the Scottish glens. On 2 July, they met at the Bridge of Alford, 27 miles from Aberdeen, where Baillie crossed the River Don while Montrose observed his manoeuvres from a ridge which dominated the river valley. Baillie was caught on boggy ground with his back to the river, but Montrose was without his trusty ally, MacDonald, who was away recruiting. Although cavalry numbers were roughly even, Montrose enjoyed an unaccustomed numerical advantage in terms of infantry.

Flanking the Royalist foot on the right was Lord George Gordon's horse, with Viscount Aboyne's horse on the left. For the Covenanters, Baillie's cavalry, under Alexander Balcarres, was deployed opposite Gordon, with the infantry ranged out to the right. Initially, the Royalists appeared to play into Baillie's hands as, with a customary disregard for discipline, Lord George Gordon's cavalry abandoned the ridge, to charge Balcarres. Apparently, Gordon was enraged by the sight of some of his own cattle which Baillie had rustled to boost provisions. Balcarres held until Nathaniel Gordon's infantry joined Lord George, using their knives to hamstring Balcarres' mounts. Aboyne's charge smashed into Baillie's right wing while Montrose led his reserves forward and Lord George Gordon rode around to the rear. Gordon's outflanking manoeuvre cost him his life for, as he was putting his hand on Baillie's sword belt, he was shot in the back and fell dead – allegedly one of only four casualties on the Royalist side. Incensed at Gordon's death, the Royalists went on the rampage, killing 700 of the enemy – and Montrose had chalked up yet another win.

South of the border, scenting total victory in the aftermath of Naseby, Fairfax was soon on his way to the south-west to tackle Goring. With so much at stake, both commanders were cautious but on 10 July, they finally came face-to-face at Langport, 14 miles to the east of Taunton. Goring arrayed his men on Ham Down, infantry to the fore, horse to the rear. Some 2,000 musketeers were deployed along the hedges bordering the narrow Langport to Somerton road. Fairfax drew up his troops opposite, on Pitney Hill, his cavalry flanked by infantry and musketeers. Fairfax had the numerical advantage, with 10,000 men opposing Goring's 8,000.

At about 11 o'clock, Fairfax decided to attack. In retrospect, this seems foolhardy. The ground on either side of the road being marshy and unsuitable for cavalry, the only way forward was along the well-defended road itself. However, Fairfax's artillery soon silenced the Royalist guns – Goring had only two of them, having sent the rest of his artillery on to Bridgwater. To clear a path for his cavalry, Fairfax sent 1,500 musketeers to deal with their Royalist counterparts. According to some accounts, the latter put up a fierce resistance, being forced to give way gradually. Other accounts suggest that many of them simply ran away.

When the hedges had been all but cleared, 400 New Model Army cavalry under the command of Major Christopher Bethel pressed forward. First, they had to descend Pitney Hill, then clear a ford at the bottom before proceeding uphill along the lane, which was wide enough to take a maximum of only four horsemen riding abreast – with the objective of taking on a strong cavalry force waiting for them on Ham Down.

Remarkably, Bethel made it, his men emerging from the lane to right and left. The will to fight seems to have deserted the Royalist cavalry, for Bethel forced them to give ground.

A counter-charge momentarily redressed the balance, but the lane was now open to allow New Model Army reinforcements through. Support in the shape of Major John Desborough appeared on the scene to consolidate Bethel's bridgehead. When Fairfax threw in his infantry and musketeers, the Royalists began to retire, some going through Langport, others making directly for Bridgwater. Hoping to delay the inevitable pursuit, those who retreated via Langport set fire to the town but Cromwell, always in at the kill, still managed to take prisoners and supplies. The retreat to Bridgwater was rather more successful, with the Royalist horse fighting an almost continuous rearguard action.

The Battle of Langport was the last large-scale battle of the Civil War. Broken and dispirited, Goring's men no longer represented a threat to the all-conquering New Model Army. Fairfax followed up with an assault on Bridgwater, which was pounded into rubble. The Royalist garrison at Bath learned from this object lesson and offered little resistance. Goring, meanwhile, withdrew to Barnstaple. His fondness for the bottle had long been remarked upon, and his most recent misfortunes launched him into a bender which had the effect of reducing the morale of his surviving troops to an all-time low.

The New Model Army now started mopping-up operations. The Royalist field armies may have been destroyed, but many strongholds stood firm. Among these were several of the great Norman castles, which had to be reduced piecemeal. One of the most important was Scarborough Castle, held for the King by Sir Hugh Cholmley since March 1643. At the beginning of 1645, Scarborough was the only North Sea port of any value remaining to the Royalists and was under siege from February to July. On 18

February, Sir John Meldrum's Parliamentarians had begun by attacking and overrunning the town, capturing 32 guns, the harbour and 120 ships. Cholmley retreated into the castle.

Meldrum dug in and ordered up some heavy guns. By sea, from Hull, came a powerful cannon, a demi-culverin called 'Sweet Lips' in honour of a celebrated local prostitute. By road, from York, came the biggest cannon in the country, the 'Cannon Royal', weighing over three tons. By the middle of March, Meldrum was ready to begin his assault but one day, while he was making his final arrangements, he fell off the cliff. It took six weeks for him to recover from his injuries. As soon as he had done so, his big guns were put to work. They did meet with success, but the garrison was still able to make an occasional successful sortie. During one of these incursions, the hapless Meldrum was hit by a musket ball, dying of his wound a few days later.

His successor, Sir Matthew Boynton, was of the opinion that enough blood had been spilt in efforts to take the castle by force. He continued the cannonade, supported by warships stationed off the headland, but he was content to starve out the defenders. Cholmley struggled on for several weeks. In the end, he was beaten by dwindling stocks of gunpowder, a shortage of water and, most of all, by scurvy – the dread disease having killed or incapacitated half the garrison. On 25 July, the survivors were allowed to march to the nearest Royalist stronghold at Newark. Cholmley himself, like the Marquess of Newcastle before him, was left penniless and boarded a ship bound for mainland Europe.

In Scotland, still on the move, still under pressure from Baillie, Montrose halted his army in low-lying meadows near Kilsyth on the evening of 14 August. Baillie advanced to occupy a commanding position to the west. Montrose had with him at least 3,000 infantry and about 500 horse. Lord George Gordon was no more, but Alasdair MacDonald had returned. Baillie may have possessed a slight numerical advantage. Reinforcements were on the way, but he was ordered to fight by representatives of the Scottish Committee of Estates, who accompanied him. His deployment is uncertain, but Balcarres' cavalry occupied the right wing, alongside the Earl of Lauderdale's infantry, with the regiments of Home and perhaps Loudon on the left. For the Royalists, Lord Ogilvy may have commanded on the right, while MacDonald certainly occupied the centre, with Nathaniel Gordon's horse and infantry on the left flank.

Baillie made the first move by despatching Major John Haldane with a party of musketeers to take the high ground to the north. Instead of acting as instructed, however, Haldane veered off to the left, towards some cottages encompassed by stone walls, which a number of Royalists had occupied. No sooner had he engaged the enemy than MacDonald rushed to the latter's aid. Attempting to re-establish control, Baillie instituted an orderly general advance, only to see Home's infantry break ranks to go to the aid of Haldane's. Initially, the ground which had become the centre of the action was not advantageous to either side, the stone walls restricting the effectiveness of Baillie's musketeers, as well as potentially destroying the impetus of any MacDonald charge. While it may have suited Baillie to sacrifice Haldane's infantry in the interests of a broader strategy, Home's intervention and the subsequent stalemate in the enclosure area now wrested the initiative away from him, placing the final outcome of the battle in the lap of the gods.

Balcarres, meanwhile, attempting to wheel round to the

north, had come under pressure from some of Gordon's horse. Again, neither side could achieve a breakthrough. It was not until Montrose threw in his reserves that Balcarres was finally overcome, exposing the Covenanter infantry regiments. The success of the horse spurred on MacDonald, his men scaling the walls to resume their attack. With Balcarres in disarray and MacDonald in full flow, the Covenanters caved in. Only a few escaped, the surviving place name of 'Slaughter Howe' bearing witness to the fate of the rest.

Two days afterwards, the Royalists entered Glasgow, MacDonald's clansmen having been expressly forbidden to pillage the city. A few, unable to restrain themselves, were executed, and MacDonald began to wonder whether his usefulness to Montrose – who was now created Marquess of Montrose – was at an end. Edinburgh was also occupied – by a single troop of horse. Only Stirling refused to bow, but this did not unduly worry Montrose who had set up court in Bothwell Palace to bask in the attention of Covenanters who came to pay their respects and profess loyalty to the King.

While the King amused himself by playing bowls at Raglan Castle, where he had retired after Naseby, Prince Rupert was at Bristol – sent there to do what he could to strengthen the defences and hold the city. He had a garrison of only 1,500 men, the city was beset by plague and morale was low, yet on 12 August, he wrote to his uncle assuring him that he could hold out for four months. Supplies were concentrated and the civilian population told to lay in provisions for six months ahead. The garrison, resolving to 'fall upon the best general defence that could be made' hoped to survive until 'the season of the year might advantage us and incommode them'.

'They' arrived on 21 August in the form of Fairfax and Cromwell with a besieging force of 12,000. They set up camp on both sides of the River Avon, the mouth of which was blockaded by a naval squadron. As might be expected, Rupert harried the besiegers to the best of his ability and Fairfax appealed to him to surrender, hinting that his name might even be deleted from Parliament's hit list. 'It would be an occasion glorious in itself, and joyful to us,' he said, 'for restoring of you to the endeared affection to the Parliament, and people of England...'

All the time, Fairfax was laying plans to storm the defences. Rupert had no intention of surrendering and Fairfax knew it. He attacked at 2 o'clock on the morning of 10 September, his heavy guns pounding Prior's Hill Fort, which Rupert had chosen for his HQ. The defenders' guns replied as the Parliamentarians stormed the Royalist line. After an hour's fierce hand-to-hand fighting, the besiegers broke through at two points. Gradually, they pressed forward to the Fort where the defenders held out until 5 o'clock. When it fell, the survivors were all put to the sword. Fairfax, often judged to be a fair, kindly man, could be ruthless when the occasion demanded, and particularly ruthless when the occasion did not demand it. He did not stand in Cromwell's way during the latter's rise to power, but Cromwell remained wary of him.

By daybreak, with Parliamentarians pouring into the streets, Rupert was no longer able to lead a co-ordinated defence. No relief could be expected, and in order to save the city, it was decided to sue for terms. It was agreed that Rupert could retain 'Colours, Pikes and Drums, Bag and Baggage' and that his men would be guaranteed safe conduct to any Royalist garrison 'not exceeding fifty miles from

Bristol'. The wounded were to be cared for in the city and the citizens protected from violence. When he heard the news, Charles was beside himself and penned a bitter letter to Rupert, advising him that, 'Though the loss of Bristol be a great blow to me, yet your surrendering it as you did is of so much affliction to me that it makes me forget not only the consideration of that place, but is likewise the greatest trial of my constancy that hath yet befallen me'. He concluded by instructing his nephew 'to seek your subsistence... somewhere beyond seas'.

True, Rupert had, indeed, promised to hold Bristol for four months. Charles even considered the possibility that the surrender had been an act of sabotage. Rupert had been advocating peace and, with the loss of Bristol, even the King must see that it would be fruitless to continue the war, so perhaps the defence had not been conducted quite as vigorously as one would have wished? Such presumptions were vague and unfounded, and it remained a cruel decision. Rupert deserved better.

Charles wrote his letter on 14 September. He did not know it, but the day before, Montrose had fought another battle – this time, at Philiphaugh, near Selkirk. So far, the year had been peppered throughout with his victories: Inverlochy in February, Auldearn in May, Alford in July, Kilsyth in August. Since Naseby, it had been in the King's mind to join Montrose. Accompanied by 2,500 troops, he had marched north in August, but was forced to turn back at Doncaster, pursued by Sir David Leslie and 4,000 cavalry. Fortunately, Leslie was recalled on receipt of the news of Kilsyth, enabling Charles to make a successful withdrawal. Leslie himself turned north where Montrose was planning to cross the border.

Even as Leslie approached Scotland, Montrose's world was falling apart. In seeking to enlist the sympathy of Covenanter supporters, he distanced himself from his Highlanders, the men who had given him his famous victories. He antagonised them further by discouraging them from plundering, and they began to drift away to their homes. Alasdair MacDonald, too, had no desire to carry the fight over the border, and parted company with his friend and ally. On 12 September, with the few hundred foot — some of MacDonald's Irish — and 200 horse remaining to him, Montrose arrived at Selkirk. He settled his infantry on a 'haugh', or stretch of low-lying land about a mile to the south-west, and ordered them to throw up a defensive ditch while he retired into the town. There was little sympathy for him here. In the house where he intended passing the night, his unwilling hostess was boiling a sheep's head. Later, she remarked that had it been Montrose's head, she would have held down the lid.

Six days earlier, Leslie had crossed into Scotland with 5,000 horse and 1,000 foot. Despite receiving reports of local enemy activity, Montrose did not believe that Leslie was anywhere in the vicinity. In fact, as he was arriving at Selkirk, Leslie was only four miles away. By making a night march under cover of mist, the Covenanters were able to surround the campsite at the haugh. When Montrose arrived on the scene, he rallied his men as best he could, massing his infantry between the ditch and his cavalry. Leslie attacked from two sides. The Irish stood their ground but, after little more than a quarter of an hour, were worn down. The story goes that just as the King was forcibly removed from Naseby, so Montrose had to be led away from Philiphaugh. The surviving infantry surrendered on the understanding that their lives would be spared. A little later, they were shot, their fate being marginally more merciful than the punishment meted out to 300 camp followers, women and children, who were hacked to pieces.

It took four weeks for confirmation of the disaster at Philiphaugh to reach the King. On 18 September, he had set out for Chester, his last remaining port and a vital landing place for Irish reinforcements. The Royalist garrison was besieged by Parliamentarians commanded by Colonel Michael Jones, but the net around the city was sufficiently slack to allow Charles and his Life Guard to slip in, while Sir Marmaduke Langdale, with his Northern Horse, made for Rowton Heath, two miles to the south east. From here, Langdale would attack Jones in the rear, while the garrison made a frontal assault It was a sound plan, spoiled by the unexpected arrival of Parliamentarian reinforcements under Major-General Sydenham Poyntz, who arrived on Hatton Heath, to Langdale's own rear.

Langdale turned to face this new threat, but he refused to budge, forcing Poyntz to make the first move. After an initial attempt to break Langdale's line ended in failure, Poyntz asked Jones for some help. Jones sent him some additional horse and a party of musketeers, who were deployed to line the hedgerows which bordered Rowton Heath. With the additional weight of horse and the fire of the musketeers, Poyntz succeeded in driving Langdale from the field. The planned assault by the garrison was repulsed and Charles had to concede that Chester was lost.

The following day, Charles left Chester to its fate, riding away with the 2,400 or so horse left to him. Somehow, he managed to reach Newark, from where he still hoped to proceed north to link up with Montrose. When news of

Montrose's defeat arrived, the remnants of Langdale's Northern Horse were despatched to Scotland to see if anything could be salvaged. To cap it all, on 16 October, Prince Rupert arrived. Accompanied by Prince Maurice, he forced his way into the King's presence, announcing that he had come to clear his name. While Charles dined, he had to suffer the indignity of his nephews standing over him and haranguing him. The next day, he granted Rupert's request for a court-martial to be convened. It found that although he was not guilty of 'the least want of courage or fidelity', he 'might have kept the castle a longer time'. It was not an exoneration, but it was all he was going to get.

In the country at large, the process of reducing the remaining pockets of Royalist resistance gathered pace. Not all the strongholds were castles; several were fortified domiciles such as Basing House in Hampshire. Home of the aged Marquess of Winchester, a leading Catholic, Basing had been under siege, on and off, for nearly two years. It was garrisoned by around 370 Royalists who had been under close confinement since August, with the arrival of Parliamentarians commanded by Colonel John Dalbier. Despite Dalbier's best efforts, Basing held out. It is said that he even used poisoned gas – setting alight bundles of damp straw soaked in arsenic, the fumes wafting over the house.

On 8 October, Cromwell appeared on the scene, bringing with him five heavy guns. Several days of concentrated bombardment followed, leading to the breach of Basing's walls in two places. On the night of 13 October, Cromwell retired to pray, seeking 'some text of Scripture to support him'. His eye fell on a text from Psalm 115 relating to idols: 'They that make them are like unto them; so is every one that putteth his trust in them.' At 6 o'clock the next morning, the Parliamentarians stormed the breaches. The battle lasted about two hours, during which about 100 of the defenders were killed, Cromwell dismissing them as 'Papists' for whom 'our muskets and swords did show but little compassion'. A number of women were killed or wounded and others 'entertained somewhat coarsely' by the victors who indulged in an orgy of looting – carrying away, it was estimated, plunder worth £250,000. The house was then set on fire, many of the surviving defenders perishing in the flames. Cromwell was in charge, and he must bear the responsibilty for the outrage.

Just a month before, he had acted with rather more decorum when dispersing a gathering of 'Clubmen' in Dorset. The Clubmen were locally organised groups of men with an agricultural base who sought to limit the depredations of the armies of both sides which lived off the land. They cared little for the politics of the Civil War and were ordinary folk trying to keep body and soul together, amid the warring factions which were intent on controlling both. Clubmen were particularly active in the south west. On 4 August, several thousand of them, led by 'two vile ministers', had gathered together on Hambledon Hill, near Shaftesbury. They were challenged by 1,000 of Cromwell's troopers, who experienced no difficulty in putting them to flight. Many escaped by sliding down the hill on their bottoms and 300 who were captured were locked up in the local church, St Mary's. Cromwell reported that a dozen Clubmen were killed, but that he had released the prisoners whom he described as 'poor silly creatures' who promised to be 'very dutiful' in future. Within two years, some of Cromwell's own colleagues within the New Model Army would be demanding that 'poor silly creatures' such as these must be given the right to vote.

1646: Checkmate

Mr Lord being always a great master of his passions... in a
pleasant humour told me that I must of necessity pawn my clothes to
make so much money as would procure a dinner.

Margaret, Duchess of Newcastle

The 1646 campaigning season opened early, with Fairfax
determined to bring the Western Royalists to book. The
Royalist Commander-in-Chief in the West was Lord
Hopton, with Lord Wentworth as Lieutenant-General of
Horse. Sir Richard Grenville, who had once occupied the
position of Commander-in-Chief, was demoted to Major-
General of Foot. Refusing to serve under Hopton, he was
arrested and imprisoned.

Towards the end of January, Fairfax besieged Exeter.
While he was thus occupied, Hopton moved north to
Torrington – scene of a minor Royalist victory in 1643 –
where he decided to make a stand, throwing up earthworks
around the town. Fairfax was happy to take the bait and,
leaving a force to continue the siege, marched to Torrington
with 10,000 men – outnumbering Hopton's army by two to
one. On 16 February, some skirmishing took place as the
Parliamentarians approached from the east, but in the failing
light of the winter afternoon, Fairfax thought it wise to
delay further action until the following morning. When

Cromwell decided to reconnoitre the Royalist defences, however, his men came under fire, and more Parliamentarian troops were brought forward in support. Thus committed to battle by the actions of his wilful subordinate, Fairfax attacked and the defenders were pushed back into the streets of Torrington.

The running fight was brought to an abrupt end by an accident. Hopton was using the Church of St Michael as a gunpowder store. Eighty barrels exploded, blowing the roof off the church and killing 200 men. Fairfax narrowly avoided becoming one of the casualties as flaming timbers, stone and molten lead rained down upon him. In the confusion, and under cover of darkness, the Royalists withdrew. It was but a temporary respite, for Hopton surrendered to Fairfax four weeks later, bringing the war in the western counties to a conclusion.

On 3 February 1646, the Royalist garrison at Chester had also fallen, dashing any lingering hopes of further succour from Ireland. The deteriorating situation within the town mirrored that of most other besieged communities. There was conflict between the military and the civil administration, the former seeking to defend the town at all costs, the latter desperate to secure long-term economic survival. Unlike the governors of other garrisoned towns, Chester's governor, Lord Byron, had refused to burn the suburbs, even though they could provide cover for an attacking force. He depended instead upon a series of earthworks. When mortars were fired into the town, the buildings caught fire anyway. According to one terrified inhabitant, these 'descending fire brands' threatened 'to set the city, if not the whole world on fire'.

In the face of stubborn resistance, the Parliamentarian

siege commander, Sir William Brereton, decided to sit it out. At length, the earthworks were captured and the defenders were reduced to shooting burning arrows into the abandoned suburban houses which now sheltered enemy snipers. It was said that a quarter of the city went up in flames. In the end, a shortage of water, food and fuel for the 7,000 people crammed within the walls, coupled with the knowledge that a relief force would not be coming, forced the garrison to sue for terms. A few armed officers and troops were permitted to march out and the safety of the public and their goods was guaranteed.

The defeat at Torrington left only one Royalist army at large. This was a 3,000-strong force led by Lord Astley (Sir Jacob had been given a peerage in November 1644) who had patched it together from survivors of regiments throughout Wales and the Midlands. When Hopton surrendered, Astley was marching from Bridgnorth to Oxford, where he planned to join the King. On 15 March, Parliamentarian Colonels John Morgan and Thomas Birch linked up at Gloucester and set out to block Astley's advance. Astley pushed on, hoping to outrun his pursuers but, on 20 March, after making a forced march of 25 miles, he was compelled to pause near the village of Donnington, about one and a half miles from Stow-on-the-Wold. That night, the Parliamentarians, strengthened by Sir William Brereton, who had been released by the capitulation of Chester, closed in. At daybreak on 21 March, they discovered that Astley was well prepared. His men were drawn up on high ground, Astley, the veteran infantryman, in the centre, flanked by Sir Charles Lucas on the right and Sir William Vaughan on the left.

The Parliamentarians advanced up the hill – Birch in the centre, Brereton on the right and Morgan on the left. At first, the Royalists stood firm, for both sides were evenly matched in terms of raw numbers and Astley had the advantage of the ground. It was the Parliamentarian horse, stronger than the Royalist horse, which turned the tide. Brereton drove Vaughan from the field and turned in on Astley's infantry, compelling them to flee into Stow-on-the-Wold. Fierce fighting continued in the streets until Astley himself was taken. His men obeyed his command to lay down their arms.

It was fitting that Astley was present at the end. He had joined the King at Nottingham in 1642 and had participated in the first major battle of the war, at Edgehill. Now, seated on a drum in the market square in Stow-on-the-Wold, he addressed his captors: 'Gentlemen,' he said, 'you have done your work and may go play, unless you will fall out among yourselves.' It was a prophetic statement.

In fact, on the wider political front, the French government was hoping to broker a deal between Charles and the Scots, whereby he would accept the terms of the Propositions of Uxbridge and surrender to Leven's army at Newark. Labyrinthine negotiations founded on this premise were conducted by a young Frenchman, Jean de Montreuil. According to Charles, Montreuil assured him that he would 'be received into the Scotch army as their natural sovereign, with freedom of my conscience and honour'. Clearly, capitulation was not on the Royal agenda.

At 3 o'clock on the morning of 23 April, with Fairfax only three days' march from Oxford, Charles stole out of his capital. Disguised as a servant, clean shaven, his hair cut short, he rode over Magdalen bridge for the last time. Making his way via Henley and Slough to Hillingdon, he half hoped to receive a message from supporters in London.

None came and he travelled on to Uppingham, which he reached on 2 May, before moving on to Southwell, arriving at the 'King's Arms' on the morning of 5 May. The meeting with the Scots, at which Montreuil officiated, took place in a room known for long afterwards as 'The French Man's Chamber'.

Charles may have been cunning, but the Scots were a great deal cannier. Having expected to be received 'with honour, safety and freedom', his disappointment must have been great when he found himself treated as a prisoner. He was told to sign the Covenant, order the establishment of Presbyterianism in England and command the surrender both of Montrose – still at large in Scotland – and of Newark's Royalist garrison. From Southwell, he was removed to Sir David Leslie's HQ at Kelham House, where he was closely guarded. The only immediate concession he made was to order Newark's surrender. He wrote to the Governor, Lord Belasyse, advising him that he was 'necessitated to march with the Scotch army this day northwards, but cannot move till this agreement be consented to by you'.

Belasyse had known of the King's imminent arrival, for he had received a letter, wrapped in a lead tube and secreted in the messenger's nether regions, informing him of the eventuality. He had not expected to be told to give in and, on receiving the order, tears came into his eyes. The Mayor of Newark urged continued resistance, to 'trust in God and sally forth', a phrase which has lived on as Newark's motto – but Belasyse obeyed the order, and Charles began his journey to Scotland.

Charles may well have wished that he had remained in Oxford and, if necessary, handed himself over to Fairfax who was, after all, 'a gentleman'. When Fairfax arrived outside Oxford and inspected the fortifications, he remarked that it was no place to be taken by what he called 'a running pull', and that 'time, hazard and industry' appeared to be the only solution. Although the garrison, 5,000 strong, was reasonably well-provisioned for a siege, Rupert thought that it could not hold out for long. Some skirmishing took place and Rupert was shot in the shoulder – miraculously the only wound he sustained in the entire war, despite having risked his life on a daily basis. Anxious 'to stop the further effusion of blood', the King had written to the governor, Sir Thomas Glemham, ordering him to surrender. On 20 June, he obeyed. Two days later, Rupert and Maurice left, with permission to remain in the country for up to six months. On 24 June, the rest of the garrison marched out, arms in hand, colours flying and drums beating.

With the fall of Oxford, it was felt that the war was now truly over, and Parliament speedily pieced together peace proposals, 'the Propositions of Newcastle', which were sent to the King at Newcastle. This time, the usual demands were more baldly stated. They were certainly thorough. For example, a law would be passed for 'the utter abolishing and taking away of all Archbishops, Bishops, their Chancellors and Commissaries, Deans and Sub-deans, Deans and Chapters, Archdeacons, Canons and Prebendaries and all Chaunters, Chancellors, Treasurers, Sub-treasurers, Succentors and Sacrists, and all Vicars Choral and Choristers, old Vicars and new Vicars... and all other under officers'. Naturally, His Majesty would 'swear and sign the late Solemn League and Covenant.'

On 1 August, Charles tendered his official response to the Propositions of Newcastle. After complaining that he had been given insufficient time to think about them, he announced that he was unable to give a considered response, as they constituted such 'great alterations in government both in the Church and kingdom'. Once again, he signalled his intention of going to London, 'where by his personal presence he may… raise a mutual confidence between him and his people', adding that he could 'never condescend unto that which is absolutely destructive to that just power which, by the laws of God and the land, he is born unto'. Even after losing a bloody civil war, his fundamental standpoint had not changed: he ruled by Divine Right and intended to continue to do so.

While these exchanges were taking place, and with no hope of relief, two Royalist castles, Pendennis and Raglan, still held out. It was said that 'Raglan and Pendennis, like winter fruit, hung long on'. Pendennis Castle, defended by the octogenarian John Arundel, was besieged by both land and sea, and was eventually starved into surrender on 16 August. Raglan Castle, held by the Marquess of Worcester, was very well defended, its walls absorbing much punishment from cannon and mortar bombardment. After the fall of Oxford, Sir Thomas Fairfax was able to strengthen the siege. Resigning himself to the inevitable, Worcester surrendered on 19 August. The garrison was well treated but, in an act of senseless vandalism, the Marquess's priceless collection of Welsh bardic manuscripts was burned. In company with many another fine fortress, the castle was then methodically destroyed.

The King's own capacity for entertaining false hope was monumental. Sooner or later, Parliament, he felt, would have to reach agreement with him. There was no other way. The thought that he might lose his head never entered it. In fact, he was increasingly being viewed as a liability by everyone with whom he hoped to form an alliance. In the main, his manoeuvrings were carried out openly, as if he were conducting a public auction at which he was selling himself to the highest bidder. He continued to entertain hopes of aid from Ireland, commanding Ormonde and others to win Irish support at any price, even to 'pawning my kingdoms for that purpose'. At one point, it was even planned to send to Ireland the Prince of Wales, who had taken refuge in Jersey, in order that he might assume command of an Irish army. However, also very active in Ireland was the Papal Nuncio, Giovanni Rinucinni. While Ormonde was busy trying to persuade the warring factions to unite and fight for their King, Rinucinni, acting on orders from Rome, was encouraging the Irish Catholics to continue to fight for their religion. Notwithstanding Rinucinni's efforts, on 30 July, Ormonde managed to bring about an agreement of sorts. Unfortunately, this had the effect of fragmenting the Irish parties even further, differences which Rinucinni was able to exploit by pointing out that in the peace treaty 'there is no mention made of the Catholic religion'. It remained very unlikely that Ireland would be rising to the occasion.

On the mainland, the threat to stability, as Astley had foreseen, came from within the victors' own ranks as wrangling over the nature of any peace settlement and the King's place in the scheme of things gathered pace. Favouring a punitive approach were the 'Independents', featuring Cromwell and Sir Arthur Haselrig, who wanted to place strict limitations on the King's future role. The New Model Army would also be preserved as insurance, in the event of Charles reneging on any agreement. A second group, including Essex and Manchester, preferred moderation in terms of a swift resolution and a return to a largely traditional form of government. At this stage, no one envisaged regicide as a solution.

There was also pressure coming from a number of fringe sects which, in time, would include Fifth Monarchists, Ranters, Sabbatarians, Socinians, Muggletonians and Sweet Singers of Israel, each with its own spiritual slant, and other groups with much broader programmes, such as the Diggers, who believed in the redistribution of land, and the Levellers, purveyors of political reform.

Most of the Levellers' demands were centuries ahead of their time. They wanted a new constitution, based on the premise that all men were equal. The monarchy and the House of Lords should be abolished, there must be frequent elections, a redistribution of parliamentary seats and an extension of the franchise, while government and the justice system should be decentralised. Radical though they might be, the Levellers would make their presence felt in the coming months.

One man who would not be present to witness future developments was the Earl of Essex, who died – it was rumoured by poison – on 16 September. The Independents refused to allow his Royalist brother-in-law, the Marquess of Hertford, to attend the funeral. Essex was buried in Westminster Abbey, and an effigy, which it is said attracted large crowds, installed in the Abbey Church. This action may be thought to be at variance with Parliament's preference for austerity as far as church furnishings were concerned. This, at least, was the opinion of a man called John White, who smashed it to pieces on the evening of 26 November, arguing that it was wrong to set up such an effigy in a sacred building.

With the approach of the first peace-time Christmas in four years, everyone should have been looking forward to the season of goodwill, but this was not the case, for Parliament had abolished festivities two years before. Attendance at special Christmas church services was banned and anyone who wanted to celebrate Christmas had to do so secretly. Eventually, even mincepies would be outlawed as symbols of excess. Prayer and fasting were the order of the day. Had men fought and died for such as this?

1647–49: Endgame

He bid me tell my mother that his thoughts had never strayed from her, and that his love should be the same to the last. Withal he commanded me and my brother to be obedient to her, and bid me send his blessing to the rest of my brothers and sisters, with commendation to all his friends.

Princess Elizabeth, daughter of Charles I, describes her last conversation with her father on the day before his execution

It says much for Charles's powers of prevarication that he was able to keep the Scots on a string for nine weary months. He made no secret about his strategy of stalling for time, supplying what he called 'handsome denying answers' to the demands made upon him, until the Scots and English fell out. In the end, the Scots grew weary of the endless sparring and resolved to remove their army from England, leaving the King behind. In effect, they sold him to the English Parliament for the sum of £400,000: a down payment of £200,000 with the balance to be paid in instalments. At the end of January 1647, Charles was handed over. Taken to Holdenby House in Northamptonshire, he must have been heartened by the show of popular support he received. On the final leg of the journey, from Market Harborough to Holdenby, the lanes were lined with cheering crowds.

With the departure of the Scots and the King in the hands

of the English Parliament, the men of the New Model Army felt that their work was done and that they, too, could return to their homes. However, one of the principles upon which the New Model Army had been formed was that of regular pay for the troops – admirable in theory, but difficult to put into practice. Arrears of £300,000 were outstanding and the New Model Army's political masters were unable to settle the bill. The New Model Army was not alone, and it has been estimated that some £2.8 million was owed to Parliamentarian troops throughout the country.

Parliament dodged and weaved: the soldiers would be paid after disbanding; the soldiers would be paid if they volunteered to serve in Ireland. During the spring of 1647, sundry mutinies broke out, but the New Model Army's discipline bore fruit, expressing itself in an unprecedented solidarity. Representatives known as 'Agitators' were elected to put the troops' grievances to their commanding officers, a process which led to the creation of a Council of the Army, with a membership comprising sympathetic general officers, two commissioned officers and two soldiers from each regiment. What they really needed, however, was a strong bargaining chip, to which end a bold plan was devised.

At Holdenby, Charles enjoyed much freedom of movement, his detention being more akin to house arrest than imprisonment. He would ride over to Harrowden Hall to play bowls with Lord Vaux, a prominent Catholic. He even managed to send and receive secret messages. On 3 June, this life of leisure was brought to an end, with the arrival of an Agitator, Cornet George Joyce, who took the King into custody. When Charles questioned his authority, Joyce merely drew attention to the 500 men accompanying him. The following day, the party proceeded to Newmarket, where the New Model Army was assembled. It was a shrewd move. With the King in its power, the New Model Army could negotiate from a position of some strength. Fairfax wanted to see Joyce called to account for his actions, but nothing was done because Joyce had acted with Cromwell's approval. From this point on, Fairfax – whether by choice or compulsion – became increasingly marginalised.

Throughout 1647, Parliament and the Army remained at loggerheads. On 15 June, the Council of the Army summarised its demands in a document entitled 'The Declaration of the Army'. Instead of concentrating on military grievances, the Army claimed that it spoke for the people. Among its demands were the dissolution of the Long Parliament, frequent general elections with parliaments of fixed duration, a degree of religious toleration, and an amnesty for most Royalists. From this beginning, the Council of the Army progressed to negotiating with the King, offering him their terms in a further document, 'Heads of the Proposals'. Based largely upon 'The Declaration of the Army', it proposed biennial elections, a redistribution of parliamentary seats and toleration of all Protestant churches, including the return of the bishops, albeit with reduced powers. Further, the Royal Family would be 'restored to a condition of safety, honour and freedom… without diminution to their personal rights, or further limitation to the exercise of the regal power'. This was a fair offer and Charles could have done worse than to throw in his lot with the Army. Instead, playing for all or nothing, he continued to stall.

By this time, cracks were appearing in the Army's solidarity. The more radical soldiers – among whom were many Levellers – resented the negotiating stance of the senior, conservative officers, or 'Grandees'. During October and November, the Council of the Army held a series of debates in the Church of St Mary the Virgin in Putney, aimed at reaching a consensus. Much of the discussion centred on the 'Agreement of the People', a Leveller document which made out a case for universal male suffrage. This demand was supported by 'The Case of the Army Truly Stated', a set of proposals formulated by 'Agitators', speaking for the common soldier.

The Grandees saw the Putney Debates as a means of limiting the revolutionary demands of the extremists, the most influential of which, by virtue of his rank, was Colonel Thomas Rainsborough, who insisted on giving the vote to all men. Rainsborough openly declared himself against the King 'or any power that would destroy God's people', reminding the gathering that although they had got the better of the Royalists in the field, they would be 'masters of our houses'. In his view, 'the poorest man in England is not all bound in a strict sense to that government that he hath not had a voice to put himself under'. What, he asked, had the common soldier fought for? Had he 'fought to enslave himself, to give power to men of riches, men of estates, to make him a perpetual slave?'

It was a sound case, but Cromwell and Ireton – who did most of the talking – argued for a franchise restricted to owners of property. Ireton admitted that he had 'an eye to property', as constituting a 'permanent interest in the kingdom... As for instance, he that hath a freehold, and that freehold cannot be removed out of the kingdom'. Cromwell felt that a decision to go any further than this 'must end in anarchy'. At length, a compromise was reached whereby servants and beggars were to be excluded from any extension of the right to vote, while soldiers who had fought for Parliament would be included. In a masterly rearguard action, however, Cromwell managed to exclude the Agitators from the closing deliberations, by which time a fresh example of the King's untrustworthiness had led to a closing of the ranks.

Charles was languishing at Hampton Court, where he had been lodged on 24 August, his position growing weaker by the minute. He even expressed fears that an attempt would be made to poison him. In November, the arrival of his daughter, Princess Elizabeth, for a visit, enabled him to hatch a plan to escape. Elizabeth was a sickly child, and Charles complained that the sound of his guards marching up and down in the middle of the night was disturbing her sleep. Obligingly, they were moved away. On 11 November, he left the building by a back staircase, crossed the river and sped away on horseback.

The first part of the King's plan – the escape itself – was masterly, but he had given little consideration to where he would go once he was out. He might have made for London where, as he had once thought, he could appeal to the populace. Alternatively, he could have sailed for Europe, from which vantage point he would have been able to organise support. Instead, he selected the Isle of Wight. Perhaps he was keeping his options open, but this was a time for bold action. He made it to the south coast and waited at Titchfield, near Fareham, while a messenger went on to the Isle of Wight to feel out its governor, Colonel Robert Hammond, a staunch Parliamentarian. Hammond went over to the mainland and, upon discovering that the King was indeed waiting, invited him over to Carisbrooke Castle, where he was kept on a loose leash.

Commissioners from both England and Scotland visited him at Carisbrooke. The English Parliament offered very little that was new. The proposals offered by the Scots, on the other hand, were more to his taste for, in return for agreeing to establish Presbyterianism in England for an initial period of three years, they would provide an army for the 'defence of His Majesty's person and authority'. Accordingly, on 26 December 1647, Scotland and the King entered into what was called their 'Engagement'.

The English Parliament had had enough and on 17 January 1648, they passed 'The Vote of No Addresses' in which they undertook to 'make no further addresses or applications to the King'. Neither would they accept any communications from him. He was also subjected to a tougher regime. The size of his household was reduced and a closer watch kept upon him. And yet, as ever, there was no shortage of folk, noble and commoner, who were prepared to risk their own lives to aid in his escape. The greater part of the resulting subterfuge involved the smuggling, in and out of the castle, of written messages.

One useful ally was the unfortunately named Jane Whorewood, daughter of one of his courtiers, to whom he wrote ciphered messages on tiny scraps of paper. It has been suggested that their content was partially pornographic in nature. According to one translation of a ciphered note, Charles promised to give Jane a 'swiving' – a contemporary term for sexual intercourse. However, it is highly unlikely that the King, the very model of moral rectitude, would ever resort to such language – or that, devoted as he was to his wife, he would entertain such a thought.

Nearer at hand, one of his ex-pages, Henry Firebrace, proved an especially useful go-between. Plans were laid for

Charles to negotiate the castle walls at a point where attendants and a horse would be waiting for him, ready to rush him to a boat and the mainland. Firebrace wanted Charles to saw through one of the bars of his chamber window, to facilitate his exit, but Charles refused and the plan failed when he got stuck in the window frame while trying to climb through it. Arrangements were made to obtain some nitric acid to help loosen the bars. In a plan of which Hammond was aware, Jane Whorewood acquired a quantity in London. It was found, together with a saw, during one of Hammond's searches. All Charles could then do was await the outcome of the 'Engagement'.

*

The fighting which occurred between May and August of 1648 is often referred to as the Second Civil War, but it would be more accurate to describe it as the death throes of the First, consisting, as it did, largely of an assortment of loosely connected localised uprisings aimed at supporting the Scottish invasion. There were many fanatics in Scotland who were against the 'Engagement'. This opposition, coupled with a shortage of funds, meant that a Scottish army was not ready to march until the summer. On 8 July, the Duke of Hamilton crossed the western border with the best force he could raise. Twelve thousand strong, it was in a bad way – on its own admission, 'without money, meal, artillery or ammunition'. Hamilton's progress was desultory and a week was spent at Kendal. His army had grown to 20,000, but the delay was invaluable to the New Model Army. The problem was not the scale of the Royalist revolt, but its diversity, which meant that the New Model Army was initially widely scattered.

On 13 August, Cromwell met with Major-General John

Lambert at Skipton. The Scots were thinly strung-out and their general situation was not helped by internal wrangling among their commanders. Their precise location was unknown but Cromwell and Lambert guessed that they might be intercepted at Preston. Luckily for them, Hamilton had, indeed, decided to march directly through Lancashire. The veteran Royalist, Sir Marmaduke Langdale, who accompanied the army, had little patience with its leisurely progress, while Hamilton's second-in-command was the Earl of Callender, with whom he did not get on. Lieutenant-General Middleton commanded the horse and General Baillie the infantry.

By 16 August, Middleton had driven south to Wigan, but Baillie's infantry was only just approaching Preston, 16 miles in the rear. The Parliamentarians spent the night of the 16 August at Stonyhurst Park, nine miles from Preston. Two-thirds of the troops were seasoned New Model Army men and, although they numbered no more than 9,000, the force they were facing was not concentrated and could therefore be addressed piecemeal. The immediate target was Langdale who, fortunately for Baillie's infantry, was on hand with his cavalry. Langdale deployed his men within a network of enclosures. Early on 17 August, the Parliamentarians attacked. Heavy rain had rendered the ground too heavy to sustain a cavalry charge and it was Lambert, armed with a pike, who led the Parliamentarian infantry in a determined assault which lasted four hours. Langdale was pushed back to the outskirts of Preston where Cromwell was able to use his cavalry, turning the retreat into a rout, crushing the reserve brigades of defenders deployed in Preston to cover Baillie's withdrawal to the south. Nightfall gave Baillie a temporary respite, for he hoped to meet Middleton's horse on their way back from Wigan to render assistance. In the darkness, the two groups missed one another.

As Baillie neared Warrington, he turned at last, but was crushed by the remorseless Parliamentarian advance. On Hamilton's orders, he surrendered the remains of his command, while Hamilton rode on into Cheshire with 3,000 horse, hoping to be reinforced by parties of local Royalists. Had he been victorious in his encounter with Cromwell, there may have been some who would gladly have ridden with him, but all potential support had melted away. On 22 August, Hamilton reached Uttoxeter, where his men mutinied. Three days later, Lambert arrived and took him into custody. The Engagers' army had been annihilated and over 10,000 prisoners taken. Those among them who had volunteered – as opposed to being pressed into service – were ultimately sent to the West Indies as slave labour. This method of disposal solved the problem of what to do with large numbers of prisoners and also acted as a deterrent. Many Royalists who were captured during the summer months shared the same fate. The victory was complete and, perhaps not undeservedly, Cromwell took the credit.

The period of renewed hostilities witnessed two major sieges – at Colchester and at Pontefract Castle. Despite the fact that they were at opposite ends of the country, they were linked by one of the most enduring mysteries of the Civil War. The Siege of Colchester won a reputation for brutality. Attempting to co-ordinate the Royalist effort in Essex were the veteran campaigners, Sir Charles Lucas and Sir George Lisle. Commanding horse and foot respectively, they made Colchester their base. In Kent, the Earl of Norwich had raised significant Royalist forces, but they suffered a heavy defeat when Fairfax opposed them at Maidstone. Norwich and 3,000 survivors marched on to London, with Fairfax in pursuit. Failing to make any impression on the capital, Norwich returned to Colchester where he joined Lucas and Lisle on 9 June. When Fairfax arrived on 13 June, he tried to storm the town. Suffering heavy losses, he was forced to withdraw.

Fairfax recognised that a siege was inevitable and began constructing a line of circumnavigation. Lucas's mansion was taken in the process and the Parliamentarians ran amok, bursting into the family vault, breaking open the coffins and, it is said, tearing apart the corpses within. When Fairfax tried to open negotiations by arranging an exchange of prisoners, Norwich refused. In retaliation, Fairfax had a number of his prisoners shot, forcing them to draw lots for the privilege.

On 5 July, Lucas and Lisle managed to break out, taking Fairfax by surprise, and succeeded in capturing guns and provisions, but the Parliamentarians regrouped quickly and cut off their line of retreat. Lucas and Lisle were able to get back into the town, but they suffered heavy casualties and lost all that they had gained in the process. The Royalists who had been wounded or taken prisoner were then set upon, robbed and killed. Fairfax claimed that this atrocity was in retaliation for Norwich's use of poisoned bullets. It seems that having run out of bespoke musket balls, the defenders were being forced to use crude substitutes fashioned from lead water pipes, but the rumour persisted.

By the middle of August, the garrison and the civilian population were reduced to eating horses. When the horse meat ran out, they ate dogs. When there were no more dogs, they ate soap and candles. Eventually, Norwich permitted some women to leave, and it was Colonel Rainsborough who ordered a number of them to be stripped naked before driving them all back inside the gates. Then, on 24 August, the garrison received the heart-rending news that Cromwell had beaten the Scots at Preston. The decision was taken to discuss terms, but Fairfax insisted that the surrender must be virtually unconditional – only what Fairfax called 'fair quarter' would be given. Lucas and Lisle were considered to fall outside the definition, and when Fairfax entered the town in triumph four days later, they were condemned to be shot. Rainsborough is sometimes blamed, but the decision was taken by the Council of the Army.

Unlike Colchester, Pontefract Castle had long enjoyed a reputation for impregnability, its defences having been the subject of continuous review and updating. Royalist garrisons had been besieged twice during 1644–45. In May 1648, a party of Royalists led by John Morris planned to recapture it – and a most valuable acquisition it would have been, had the Scots managed to drive south. Morris planned a bloodless coup, for he had confederates on the inside, one of whom was a corporal who promised to turn a blind eye during guard duty while Morris and 80 Royalists erected scaling ladders against the castle walls. At the agreed time, the corporal, having imbibed freely, was the worse for wear and a less sympathetic colleague caught Morris in the act. The ladders fell into the castle's formidable ditch and the Royalists fled.

In view of this scare, it was decided to strengthen the Parliamentarian garrison, which numbered only about thirty, with some additional troops billeted in the town. In readiness, the Governor, Colonel Overton, requisitioned supplies, including a number of extra beds. On 3 June, some carts bearing the beds, and accompanied by Morris with some of his Royalists disguised as removal men, arrived at the main gate. The guards were given some drinking money and sent away, leaving the Royalists free to overpower the remainder of the slender garrison, all of whom, including Overton, were thrown into the dungeons. Morris was given the rank of Colonel and ushered in as the new Royalist Governor. The castle was well provisioned with food and ammunition, but a steady influx of sympathisers compelled Morris to lay in additional supplies by mounting several local raids. It was just as well, because he was soon besieged by 5,000 Parliamentarian regulars, commanded by Sir Henry Cholmley, brother of the Sir Hugh Cholmley who had held Scarborough Castle for the King.

Despite his strength, Sir Henry conducted a very slack siege. The garrison appears to have experienced no trouble in importing foodstuffs, driving in several hundred head of cattle and even fraternising with the Parliamentarian troopers to the extent of selling them horses. When news reached Fairfax, he arranged for Cholmley to be relieved of his command. The man he sent to replace him was Colonel Rainsborough, villain of the piece at Colchester and dedicated left-winger. When Rainsborough arrived on 17 October, Cholmley wrote to Parliament, complaining of the indignity of having 'one put over us that is but a bare Colonel of Foot... and a younger colonel than any of us'. Rainsborough insisted that Cholmley hand over command, but the difficulty was resolved on the morning of Sunday 29 October, when Rainsborough himself was found dead in the street.

The circumstances of Rainsborough's death are shrouded in mystery. His lodgings were in Doncaster, where he awaited orders from Fairfax as to whether he should take over from Cholmley or go elsewhere. Out of consideration for the town, he retained only two companies of his men there, billeting the rest of his infantry in the surrounding villages. At around 8 o'clock on the morning of 29 October, a party of Royalists from Pontefract Castle, 47 in number, rode into Doncaster, explaining to a single man at the main guard post that they bore fresh orders from Cromwell. The Captain of the Guard was not present – and afterwards claimed that his absence had been occasioned by illness. Twenty-two of the Royalists made for Rainsborough's lodgings, and the sentry allowed two of them – each holding a pistol – to enter. Dragging Rainsborough from his bed, they bundled him down the stairs and tried to force him to mount a horse. He refused, saying that he would 'die in that place rather than go with them'. Then, while the sentry stood by and watched, they ran him through with their swords. As they rode away, they turned to see him on his feet, staggering after them, before falling to the ground. Returning, they ran him through several more times.

According to Morris, the plan was his. It had been the aim of the expedition to capture Rainsborough and hold him hostage for the safe return of Sir Marmaduke Langdale, captured after Preston, who, it was feared, would share the fate of Lisle and Lucas. Apparently, the party returned safely to the castle, with 50 prisoners in tow. Rainsborough's death was very convenient for Cromwell and Fairfax, neither of whom could stomach his revolutionary ideals. Although siege operations had been inadequate, Cholmley must have tightened them up in the hope of being able to hold onto his command, and it would not have been easy for 47 horsemen to ride out, complete the 24-mile round trip and return safely with an additional 50 men. What of the fortuitous absence of the Captain of the Guard and the curious lack of support from Rainsborough's own men? And how had his assailants known that Rainsborough was expecting a message?

As with all conspiracy theories, the possibilities are endless. At worst, it had been an inside job, arranged by Cromwell with or without the connivance of Fairfax. Cholmley had allowed the party to pass through his lines, and the Doncaster town guard had been told not to interfere. Alternatively, the task of taking over the siege could have been allotted to Rainsborough simply as a means of getting him out of the way. Even here, there are difficulties. His robust methods had succeeded at Colchester, and perhaps he was chosen as the man most likely to finish what could otherwise turn out to be a lengthy siege. Most tellingly for the conspiracy theorists, despite the enmity which had existed between himself and Rainsborough, Cromwell managed to get himself put in charge of the subsequent investigation ordered by Parliament. In the event, Pontefract held out until 23 March 1649 – arguably a largely academic exercise, considering the momentous events of January 1649.

The King's hopes were dashed. On 18 December, he was removed from Carisbrooke, by which time he was a pitiable sight. His hair and beard were long and unkempt, for he would not let a barber near him in case his throat was cut. He was a small man, barely five feet in height, and when they came for him, they found a shrunken, dishevelled creature – but any suspicions that his spirit might be broken were soon to be dispelled. He was taken to Newport where, despite The Vote of No Addresses, negotiations with Parliament were resumed. Upon giving his word not to attempt to escape, he was permitted to have contact with friends and advisors. It was better than he could have hoped for, considering the extent of his duplicity. He made a number of concessions, consenting once more to the introduction of Presbyterianism for an initial three-year period and agreeing to let Parliament settle matters in Ireland. And still his nature got the better of him. He corresponded with the Queen on the possibility of an Irish uprising and continued to listen to various ideas for his escape – all of which were known to Hammond.

Yet, time was running out. Having restored order, the Army was once more turning its attention to the political arena. The King, it decided, had to go. It would be folly to trust him any longer. Even if it had been possible to reach an accommodation, it was certain that he would ditch it at the earliest opportunity. There was no other way. In the 'Remonstrance of the Army', presented to Parliament on 20 November, the demand was made that Charles must be 'brought to justice for the treason, blood and mischief' of which he was guilty. Parliament deferred its consideration of the document and in so doing sealed its own fate as well as that of the King.

On 6 December, Members of Parliament arriving at the House of Commons were met at the entrance by troops commanded by Colonel Thomas Pride. In his hands, Pride held a list of 143 Members who were considered unsympathetic to the Army. Anyone named on the list was sent packing. Most obeyed and those who did not were placed under arrest. Cromwell claimed that he had not been 'acquainted' with the action, although it had been set in motion on the orders of his son-in-law, Ireton. Also in ignorance of the plan was Fairfax who appeared to know very little of what was happening in his own army. Had he taken a stronger lead at the outset, events might have taken a different turn, but he had allowed himself to be reduced to little more than a figurehead, an unwilling stooge in whose name Cromwell and Ireton could construct the foundations of their New Jerusalem.

Meanwhile Charles was housed at Hurst Castle for two weeks before being removed to Windsor Castle, where he arrived on 23 December to join other Royalist prisoners, including the Duke of Hamilton. Here he remained – no longer the king, but merely 'Charles Stuart' – while his captors decided whether he should live or die. One final overture was made to him, offering him restoration on condition that he accepted the supremacy of Parliament. He refused.

The purged Parliament, which would become known as the 'Rump Parliament', consisted of no more than 80 members – its function now to legalise the Army's directives. An ordinance was passed for the creation of a High Court of Justice to try 'Charles Stuart' on the basis that 'by the fundamental laws of England, it is High Treason for a King to levy war against his Parliament and Kingdom'. The trial was little more than a public show staged to 'legalise' his execution. Cromwell remained in the background and it fell to John Bradshaw as Lord President of the High Court of Justice to oversee the proceedings, which lasted three working days during 20-23 January 1649. As the Solicitor-General, John Cook read the charges, Charles tried to interrupt, tapping Cook, on the arm with his silver-topped cane. Cook ignored him, but the head of the cane fell off, an ill-omen – like the collapse of the Standard at Nottingham – with an implication that cannot have been lost on anyone.

The trial itself consisted of the case for the prosecution,

with the King continually denying the legality of the court. He refused to plead in answer to the charges, seeking to know 'by what power I am called hither', adding that he was his accusers' 'lawful King... with a trust committed to me by God, by old and lawful descent'. His stance had not changed at all and Cromwell must have felt justified. When it came to be uttered, the sentence was no less shocking for being expected: that 'Charles Stuart, as a Tyrant, Traitor, Murderer and a public enemy shall be put to death, by the severing of his head from his body.' Amid tumult on the final day, the King was led away to Whitehall.

Fifty-nine signatures were appended to the death warrant. Most of the regicides had signed willingly although, at the Restoration, many would claim that they had done so under duress. Among their number was a sprinkling of well-known names: Cromwell and Ireton; Bradshaw and Cook; Colonels Thomas Pride, John Okey, who had fought at Naseby, and Valentine Walter, whose son had died at Marston Moor. Others were rank and file Parliamentarians, back-room boys whose commitment to the cause would cost them dear: Henry Smith, Leicestershire MP, would be sentenced to life imprisonment at the Restoration and die in Jersey's Queen Elizabeth Castle; Augustine Garland, Member for Queenborough in Kent, condemned to transportation for life; Gregory Clement, Member for Fowey, hanged, drawn and quartered.

The night before his execution, Charles bade farewell to his children, Princess Elizabeth and the eight-year-old Prince Henry, the only two still left in England. 'They are going to cut off your father's head,' he told them. The following morning was bitterly cold and he put on two shirts, one over the other, in case he shivered and people thought he was afraid to die. He was made to walk over to Whitehall and, when he arrived, had to wait because no one could be found to perform the execution.

At length, when he mounted the scaffold, he discovered that the spectators had been placed too far away to hear his last words. And yet, he spoke, referring to a scrap of paper upon which he had scribbled a few notes. In an obvious reference to his sacrifice of Strafford, he pronounced, 'An unjust sentence that I suffered to take effect, is punished now by an unjust sentence on me.' In justification of his political stance, he assured the people that he desired 'their liberty and freedom as much as anybody' but that liberty and freedom had little to do with having a share in government. 'That,' he said, 'is nothing pertaining to them.' In justification of his religion, he averred that he died a Christian, 'according to the profession of the Church of England, as I found it left me by my father'.

His head was severed from his body by a single blow of the axe, wielded, it was rumoured, by Cornet Joyce, the man who had taken him into custody at Holdenby. The crowd was quickly dispersed and the corpse carried back into the palace to await embalming. During the night, a cloaked figure paid a secret visit to the coffin and stood over it for a while before muttering the words, 'Cruel necessity!' It was Cromwell.

The monarchy was abolished by Act of Parliament. The King, it was proclaimed on 17 March, had been 'put to death for many treasons, murders and other heinous offences'. The office of King was adjudged to be 'unnecessary, burdensome, and dangerous to the liberty, safety, and public interest of the people'. It was therefore ordained that 'the office of a King in this nation shall not henceforth reside in or be exercised by any one single person' – the abolition ensuring that 'a most happy way is made for this nation to return to its just and ancient right, of being governed by its own representatives... chosen and entrusted for that purpose by the people.'

On 25 May 1657, less than a decade after Charles's execution, Parliament was to ask Cromwell to accept the Crown.

Appendix
English Civil War Timeline

1638

27 February Scottish National Covenant
12 June Conclusion of John Hampden's trial

1639

March-June First Bishops' War
19 June Pacification of Berwick

1640

13 April Meeting of Short Parliament
July-October Second Bishops' War
28 August Alexander Leslie defeats Lord Conway at the Battle of
Newburn
26 October Treaty of Ripon
3 November First Meeting of Long Parliament
11 December Root and Branch Petition

1641

15 February Triennial Act
12 May Execution of Earl of Strafford
5 July Court of Star Chamber abolished
7 August Ship Money abolished
22 October Irish Rebellion
1 December The Grand Remonstrance

1642

4 January The King attempts to arrest the 'Five Members'

10 January The King leaves London

23 February Queen Henrietta Maria sails for Holland

23 April The King is refused entry to Hull

1 June The Nineteen Propositions

22 August Royal Standard raised at Nottingham

23 September Prince Rupert defeats Captain Fiennes at Powick Bridge

23 October The King claims victory over the Earl of Essex at Edgehill

29 October The King enters Oxford

13 November Stand-off between the King and Essex at Turnham Green

1643

18 January Sir Ralph Hopton defeats Colonel Ruthin at Bradock Down

1 February Treaty of Oxford

22 February Queen Henrietta Maria lands at Bridlington

19 March The Earl of Northampton defeats Sir John Gell at Hopton Heath

30 March Goring defeats Sir Thomas Fairfax at Seacroft Moor

16 May Hopton defeats the Earl of Stamford at Stratton

18 June Prince Rupert defeats Parliamentarians at Chalgrove

30 June Newcastle defeats Lord Fairfax at Adwalton Moor

5 July Hopton defeats Sir William Waller at Lansdown

13 July Hopton defeats Waller at Roundway Down

2 September-12 October Siege of Hull

20 September Earl of Essex defeats the King at Newbury

25 September Solemn League and Covenant

11 October Earl of Manchester defeats Sir William Widdrington at Winceby

8 December Death of John Pym

1644
19 January Scottish army crosses the border
25 January Sir Thomas Fairfax defeats Lord Byron at Nantwich
16 February Committee of Both Kingdoms
29 March Waller defeats Hopton at Cheriton
11 April Lord Fairfax defeats Sir John Belasyse at Selby
22 April-16 July Siege of York
29 June The King defeats Waller at Cropredy Bridge
2 July Leven defeats Prince Rupert at Marston Moor
14 July Queen Henrietta Maria sails for France
28 August Earl of Montrose raises the Royal Standard in Scotland
31 August The King defeats the Earl of Essex at Lostwithiel
1 September Montrose defeats Lord Elcho at Tippermuir
13 September Toleration Order
27 October Drawn battle between the King and Manchester at Newbury
24 November Propositions of Uxbridge

1645
10 January Execution of Archbishop Laud
2 February Montrose defeats Marquess of Argyll at Inverlochy
17 February New Model Army Ordinance
3 April Self-Denying Ordinance
9 May Montrose defeats Hurry at Auldearn
14 June Fairfax defeats the King at Naseby
2 July Montrose defeats Baillie at Alford
10 July Fairfax defeats Goring at Langport
15 August Montrose defeats Baillie at Kilsyth
11 September Prince Rupert surrenders Bristol
13 September Sir David Leslie defeats Montrose at Philiphaugh
24 September General Poyntz defeats the King at Rowton Heath

1646

16/17 February Fairfax defeats Hopton at Torrington
21 March Sir William Brereton defeats Lord Astley at Stow-on-the-Wold
5 May The King surrenders to the Scots at Southwell
6 May Surrender of Newark
24 June Surrender of Oxford
13 July Propositions of Newcastle

1647

26 January The King handed over to Parliament
13 March Surrender of Harlech Castle
16 May Declaration of the Army
4 June The Army removes the King from Holdenby House
1 August The Heads of the Proposals offered by the Army
24 August The King sent to Hampton Court
28 October The Agreement of the People
28 October – 8 November The Putney Debates
11 November The King escapes from Hampton Court
26 December The Engagement between the King and the Scots

1648

11 February Vote of No Address
3 June-24 March 1649 Siege of Pontefract Castle
13 June-27 August Siege of Colchester
17/18 August Scots and English Royalists defeated at Preston
6 December Pride's Purge

1649

30 January Execution of the King
7 February Abolition of the monarchy

Bibliography

Coward, Barry, *Stuart England 1603–1714*, Harlow: Longman, 1997

Firth, CH *Cromwell's Army*, London: Greenhill Books, 1992

Fraser, Antonia, *Cromwell Our Chief of Men*, London: Mandarin, 1989

Gardiner, SR *A History of the Great Civil War Vols I-IV*, Witney, Oxfordshire: Windrush Press, 2002

Hibbert, Christopher, *Charles I: A Life of Religion, War and Treason*, Basingstoke: Palgrave Macmillan, 2007.

Hunt, Tristram, *The English Civil War: At First Hand*, London: Weidenfield & Nicolson, 2002

Kenyon, John & Ohlmeyer, Jane, *The Civil Wars: A Military History of England and Scotland 1638–1660*, Oxford: Oxford University Press, 1998

Plowden, Alison, *Women All On Fire: The Women of the English Civil War*, Stroud, Gloucestershire: Sutton Publishing, 2000

Purkiss, Diane, *The English Civil War: A People's History*, London: HarperCollins, 2007

Reid, Stuart, *All the King's Armies*, Staplehurst, Kent: Spellmount Press, 1998

Royle, Trevor, *Civil War: Wars of the Three Kingdoms 1638–1660*, London: Abacus, 2005

Websites

www.caliverbooks.com (specialist English Civil War
booksellers)
www.battlefieldstrust.com
www.cromwell.argonet.uk (The Cromwell Association)
www.sealedknot.org
www.english-civil-war-society.org.uk
www.british-civil-wars.co.uk
www.scotwars.com
www.ecwsa.com (The English Civil War Society of
America)
www.english-heritage.org.uk

Index of People and Places

THE ROYALL

Sero sed Serio.

Quo

Kill and take posses=
sion 1. Kings. 19.

Barathrum Ejus
Charibdis Vectigalium

ΕΙΚ
ΩΝ
ΕΑΣ
ΙΛΙΚΗ

Let us kill him and seyse
Inheritance Math 21. 38

Defæcates manus ibi fas vbi maxima me

Lex trum

Lupus